Game Design Deep Dive

Game Design Deep Dive

Roguelikes

Joshua Bycer

CRC Press
Taylor & Francis Group
Boca Raton London New York

CRC Press is an imprint of the
Taylor & Francis Group, an **informa** business

First edition published 2021
by CRC Press
6000 Broken Sound Parkway NW, Suite 300, Boca Raton, FL 33487-2742

and by CRC Press
2 Park Square, Milton Park, Abingdon, Oxon, OX14 4RN

© 2021 Joshua Bycer

CRC Press is an imprint of Taylor & Francis Group, LLC

ISBN: 978-0-367-71371-3 (hbk)
ISBN: 978-0-367-63819-1 (pbk)
ISBN: 978-1-003-15053-4 (ebk)

Typeset in Minion
by Deanta Global Publishing Services, Chennai, India

Dedication

I would like to dedicate this book to my late grandfather Herbert Pousman, who died in 2015. He was always a supporter of my work and one of the kindest souls in my life. Unfortunately, he left us before I became an author, and I could not share my book with him, and this is a small way of being able to honor him.

Contents

Preface

Welcome to my second book in the *Game Design Deep Dive* series. When I started this with *Game Design Deep Dive: Platformers* (Taylor & Francis, 2020), I purposely chose the most recognizable and long-lasting genre in the game industry.

For this entry, we are going to examine a genre that had remained a niche sensation for over 30 years. Roguelike design presents a rich canvas for designers to play around with, leading to even arguments over the genre definitions. This is a genre that has as much potential as it does pitfalls for designers that do not understand its quirks.

The last decade saw the genre and its design philosophy become one of the most popular examples of games, besides platformers, for indie developers to make. In that same span of time, developers have experimented with roguelike elements in other genres to create totally unique designs.

Another reason I wanted to write about roguelikes is the use of procedural and random generation and to clear up misconceptions about the practice. Being able to create a game that can design content is one of the hardest aspects of game design, and there are not enough formal discussions about it.

Writing this book gave me a chance to focus the last decade of thinking about roguelikes into a single source, and I hope this will provide some useful knowledge for new and existing developers.

As always, please let me know what you think either on Twitter @GWBycer or at josh@game-wisdom.com.

Acknowledgments

For each one of my books, I run a donation incentive for people to be acknowledged. Here are the people who helped support me while I was writing *Game Design Deep Dive: Roguelikes*:

Christen Bacheler
Michael Berthaud
D.S
Thorn Falconeye
Adriaan Jansen
Jonathan Ku
Robert Leach
Aron Linde
Josh Mull
Rey Obomsawin
Onslaught
Adam Petrone
David Pittman
Puppy Games
Sharky

Author

Joshua Bycer is a game design critic with more than seven years of experience critically analyzing game design and the industry itself. In that time, through Game-Wisdom, he has interviewed hundreds of game developers and members of the industry about what it means to design video games. He is also a public speaker and presenter at schools and libraries on game design and game development.

1

Introduction

Even though my first love of videogames is of action-based games, **roguelikes** have become a close second. While I played a few of them when I was younger, it was not until the 2010s that I embraced the genre, and I have been playing every variety of them since.

For this deep dive, we are going to explore the history and design of the genre and its many nuances. Despite the flood of titles from indie developers, it is an extremely hard genre to do properly.

When I was first exposed to roguelikes, I remember writing on my original blog in 2008 about how the term **replayability** was going to become an important aspect of game development. Since then, I have been proven right, with the mainstream growth of roguelike design and building games around **live-service** design. However, many developers do not understand the amount of work and complexity that is required to create a game that keeps the consumer coming back for more. Live-service design could easily fill its own book in terms of practices and philosophies from around the industry.

In the last decade, the concept of a roguelike has changed dramatically, and the genre in its many forms has become a popular option for indie developers. There are misconceptions about roguelike design that we are going to tackle in this book that are often issues we see from first attempts by developers. But perhaps the hardest goal of this book is to finally give a definitive answer to this question: "what is a roguelike?" and how the definition for the genre has changed over the past 30 years.

We are also going to bring up three different games that were featured in my first book *20 Essential Games to Study* (Taylor & Francis, 2019), and there is a reason for that. Each game, in a way, not only changed game design forever but left lasting marks on the industry that other developers would soon emulate and grow from. Also, each game was completely different from the others in the roguelike elements their designs explored.

I was not originally going to write my third book on roguelikes but on horror; however, in 2019, the signs were there with so many roguelike and roguelike-inspired games being released that it felt like this was the right time. Confusion over the designs and definitions of the genre still exists, and as with platforming, there is a wide line between good and bad takes.

The parallels between roguelikes and platforming do not stop there. There are so many roguelikes on the market today that just making a good one is not enough to stand out, just like platformers. And with that, let us start where roguelikes began.

2

The Birth of the Rogue

2.1 Early Rogues

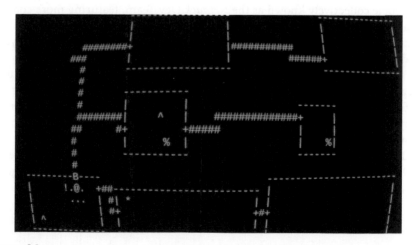

Figure 2.1

Early roguelikes like Nethack would set the foundation of roguelike design to this very day.

Whenever we talk about the origins of genres and designs, we should remember that the game industry is notoriously bad at keeping exact dates and designating games as "the first" of their genre. With the rise of videogames and computer games in the 1970s, developers were beginning to create new experiences. Early role-playing games (**RPGs**) were text-based: Using only text and no art to tell a story (Figure 2.1).

In 1974, the very first edition of *Dungeons and Dragons* by Gary Gygax and Dave Arneson, a pen-and-paper tabletop RPG, was released and would begin fans' long-lasting love of fantasy settings. The reason why these titles were important was that they helped to inspire what would become the game that set the standard for roguelike **gameplay**: *Rogue*.

Rogue was originally developed by Michael Toy and Glenn Wichman and technically released in 1980. The reason for "technically" is because the first version of the game was never sold but distributed among fans for free. *Rogue* embodied all the aspects that would become standard for roguelikes that we will talk about in the next section.

Sadly, despite being the game that would become synonymous with the genre, *Rogue* never became a commercial success. A commercial version worked on by Toy was released in 1984 which did not perform well in the market. The main reasons were because the free version of *Rogue* was still available and because the game went on to inspire several notable titles that were also free. Two of the most popular roguelikes at the time were *Hack*, made by Jay Fenalson and released in 1982 (and then expanded by Andries Brouwer in 1984), and *Moira* by Robert Koeneke in 1983.

Hack was an original roguelike where the objective was to find the amulet of Yendor hidden at the bottom of a dungeon. The game generated the floors at startup, and they remain consistent for the length of the play.

Hack was eventually re-released in the form of *Nethack* in 1987 by a group of people collectively known as the *Nethack* Dev Team, featuring more content, challenges, and things to do. *Nethack* is considered by fans to be one of the best roguelikes ever made and is still being worked on and updated after over 30 years of development and can be found for free online.

Moira was a roguelike built around the *Lord of the Rings* setting and featured larger levels than *Hack* at the time and was centered on reaching the Balrog and defeating it. Unlike *Hack*, *Moira* generates new levels during play whenever the **player** moves to a new floor. *Moira* is now open source and available under the name *Umoira*.

Even though the term **roguelike** would not get coined until around the early 1990s, these classic games would form the basis of what the roguelike genre means to its fans.

2.2 What Is a Roguelike Like?

We will be coming back to this question throughout this book, as it has taken on new meaning with the growth of the roguelike genre. Let us go over the basic definition and elements that stayed true for more than 20 years. In the next chapter, we will start looking at these points more closely.

The roguelikes of the 1980s shared common elements and designs. Each title was built on RPG **systems** where in-game **characters** would find new gear and grow more powerful over the course of playing. Players would always start these games by building a character. Typically, these games had multiple races or classes that would determine starting attributes and abilities. All gameplay occurred in a **turn-based** system – where the game only moves forward after the player inputs a command (Figure 2.2).

What separated roguelikes from other games was the use of random and **procedurally generated content**.

When people think about a videogame, they view them as a linear experience that is played through once and then finished. The roguelike genre was the first to generate content each time someone played the game. This included the environments, enemy and item placements, and much more.

Because there was no set design of roguelikes, early developers needed to do something different to represent the game on screen. Instead of creating art **assets**, roguelike developers used the programming language **ASCII**. Everything in the game was assigned a symbol used in ASCII, which turned into a low-cost method for designing a game without requiring extensive art. One of the more famous examples would be the hit game *Dwarf Fortress* by Tarn and Zach Adams of Bay 12 Games, first released in 2006, which also makes use of generating content.

To add a greater sense of challenge for the player, roguelikes featured a concept known as **permadeath**. When the player's character dies in a roguelike,

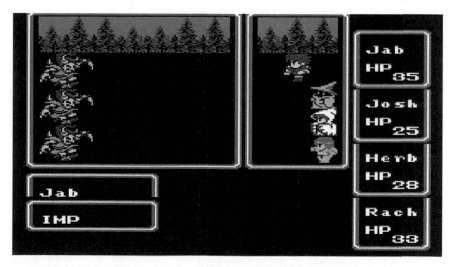

Figure 2.2

Role playing and strategy games popularized turn-based strategy design.

their character and save file are deleted, which requires them to restart the game completely. Instead of letting the player manually save their game, roguelikes would save after every action, preventing the player from undoing a mistake or bad event. We will discuss the use and popularity of permadeath more in the next chapter.

Depending on the game, some roguelikes would allow a sense of carryover or **persistence** across runs. When the character died, future playthroughs could have the remains and items of a previously killed character.

Despite the advanced design of roguelikes, it would take a growth of the term and gameplay, and about 30 years in the market, before the mainstream began to fully appreciate it. With that said, it is time to talk about the basics of roguelike design.

3

Basic Roguelike Design

3.1 Turn-Based Design

Turn-based gameplay makes up multiple genres of games which are beyond the scope of this book, but the basics are important to understand for roguelike designers. As we mentioned, turn-based design means that the gameplay is essentially "frozen" while the player is deciding what to do. This accommodates players who do not have twitch reflexes and has always rewarded careful thinking as opposed to quick reactions.

The two most popular forms of turn-based gameplay are colloquially referred to as "I-Go-You-Go" and "We-Go." I-Go-You-Go means that characters take their turns one at a time. The easiest implementation is separating the players' characters from the opposing enemies. One side performs all their actions and then the other side will perform their actions. This structure provides an easy to understand breakdown of how combat plays out and has been a staple of strategy and tactical games, like the *XCOM* franchise (first released in 1994) by MicroProse, for years (Figure 3.1).

Advanced versions of this system broke this down further into individual characters, determining who goes first based on specific rules defined by the design.

Figure 3.1

The XCOM franchise has endured, thanks to its challenging turn-based design and long-form campaign structure.

Oftentimes, these games will represent the order via a timeline: giving the player an idea of who is going next so they can plan their actions around it.

A We-Go system means every character who is active will perform an action at the same time. Oftentimes, this allows enemy characters to chase the player's character down, as every step the player takes, the enemy will follow suit. We-Go design is usually only seen in roguelikes that focus on a single playable character.

The one exception is the **subgenre** of strategy games known as "simultaneous turn-based strategy." For these games, every player performs all the actions they can during a turn and submits them to the game. Once all the turns have been collected, the game will run, taking all the commands issued and letting the players see the results of their actions. This kind of design has become a popular multiplayer option for fans of turn-based strategy games and is used in the system known as "Play by Email" (**PBEM**).

Play by Email, as a side benefit, gets around the need to set up a multiplayer architecture for a title, as the players are not playing at the same time. Either the game uploads and downloads the turns for all the players, or each player must do it manually.

Turn-based design from a gameplay standpoint is easier to work with compared to **real-time** games. The limitations of the turns mean that every player is operating the game the same way, with no player getting an inherent advantage. As we will talk about throughout this book, it does present challenges in terms of balance and pacing when changing, even just one value could affect every part of the design.

3. Basic Roguelike Design

3.2 The Failure Loop

Roguelikes have always been defined by their difficulty and the challenge of winning. A key element of the **core gameplay loop** is the fact that players are going to be losing repeatedly and starting over.

The act of losing all progress was one of the reasons that kept roguelikes from mainstream markets outside of a few exceptions. Roguelikes are all about learning and mastering the rules of their systems. A good player will learn through failure the ins and outs of playing and use that knowledge on future runs. Expert players of a roguelike who understand all the rules governing the game can oftentimes mitigate the randomness of each run. With that said, the randomness is at the heart of the roguelike genre, and players can still end up losing if everything goes wrong (Figure 3.2).

A major aspect of playing a roguelike is being able to assess the risks of any action the player takes. One of the more popular elements of roguelike games is having set events or items that can show up but having the results of using them be randomized. Drinking a red potion in one play may recover health but could just as well poison the character on a different run.

Items generated could also have random effects attached to them. Many items would drop as being "unidentified," and would not tell the player if they had good or bad modifiers on them. Players would have to normally use a secondary item to identify them, or just use the item and see what the results are.

The difficulty and focus on failure for roguelikes take us to the first misconception outsiders have about roguelike design: "Roguelikes are only about punishing the player." All roguelikes are built on rules that govern how the game works and leave it to the player to figure them out.

Figure 3.2

Roguelikes are not as punishing as people think.

As we have talked about, the chances of someone brand new winning a rogue-like on their very first run is astronomically low. Master-level play comes down to exploiting the rules and systems to give the player the best chance at winning.

The other part of the argument has to do with permadeath and how it can be viewed as a horrible punishment. The next two sections of this chapter are going to focus on why, even though the player loses everything when they fail, it is not considered that painful of an experience.

3.3 Replayable Gameplay

Roguelikes were the first genre to be built on the concept of replayability or making a game that can be replayed multiple times. Replayability has become a major goal of live-service games to ensure that players keep coming back, and of course, spend money.

A good roguelike is one that is not finished after the player has beaten it one time. There is a lot to designing a replayable game beyond just roguelike design, especially with **free-to-play** games that we do not have the space here to explore.

For roguelikes, the replayability occurs in several ways. As we talked about in the previous section, the fact that permadeath wipes the player's progress guarantees that they are going to be replaying the game by design (Figure 3.3).

What keeps a roguelike interesting for fans is the use of random and procedural generation to create entirely different runs with each play. We will be spending Chapter 5 of this book discussing generating content at length.

Figure 3.3

Dying just means being able to play the game again with a different experience.

Even the most seasoned player of a roguelike will never know exactly what to expect when they start a new game. The length of a typical play can vary based on the design of the roguelike, but no matter how long a play is, it is going to be different from the previous one. That sense of having to adapt at a moment's notice to what is happening has been one of the strongest features of roguelike design.

Modern roguelikes often make use of persistent systems that add new content the more someone plays – further incentivizing repeated plays – which is a concept that will be discussed fully in Section 6.6.

For consumers who are not used to roguelike design, they may be wondering why the concept of permadeath, or a "hardcore" mode, is a staple of the genre.

3.4 The Appeal of "Hardcore" Mode

Roguelikes were the genre that popularized permadeath, but it has also been used in other genres. Hardcore difficulty is the term that is used by developers to let the player know that death or failure is permanent. Despite originating with roguelikes that generate new runs, we have even seen linear games make use of permadeath – such as *Doom* (2016) and 2020's *Doom Eternal* by Id Software with their "Ultra Nightmare" difficulty setting.

It is hard to give a definitive answer for why hardcore difficulty is still popular among fans, as everyone has different tastes. Having the entire playthrough at risk gives the game a different feel when players know that there are consequences for messing up (Figure 3.4).

Figure 3.4

Permadeath can keeps things exciting and always requires the player to stay on their toes.

Personally, when I play action role-playing games (**ARPGs**) without the threat of losing a character, they become boring to play. I know that there are no penalties and can keep banging my head against a wall until I win.

As we have talked about, roguelikes are built on generating content to make each playthrough feel different. Restarting a roguelike should mean getting a new experience, something that does not happen in linear games.

Going back to *Doom* and *Doom Eternal*, I do not feel the same way about permadeath for them compared to roguelikes. In a linear game, success is about proper execution and knowing exactly what the game throws at the player. In my previous book *Game Design Deep Dive Platformers*, we spoke about **Kaizo** games – titles featuring exceedingly difficult levels that can only be beaten by perfect play. These games are not about adapting to any changes but mastering a highly precise set of instructions to win.

Some games will offer unique rewards for playing on hardcore difficulty. A popular option is having a ranking or ladder system that rates players on how far they can go before their character is killed. A unique exception to permadeath and hardcore mode would be Grinding Gear Games' *Path of Exile*, released in 2013. Instead of killing a character in hardcore mode, the game shifts the character into the normal mode to allow players to keep playing them, albeit without the reward or distinction for hardcore play.

For our next chapter, we are going to focus on the games that integrated different aspects of roguelike design in the 1990s and 2000s.

4

Off-Brand Roguelikes

4.1 *Toejam and Earl*

Figure 4.1

The latest entry of Toejam and Earl was aimed at rebooting the series and reestablishing the roguelike nature.

Roguelikes retained a hardcore fanbase on the PC for decades, but it wasn't until changes and major steps forward in the 2010s that the genre became more mainstream. Before then, we saw several franchises who have experimented with roguelike designs, while not necessarily referring to themselves as roguelikes, or in some cases, not being considered as such by fans.

The first of these would be *Toejam and Earl*, released in 1991 (Figure 4.1). Created by Greg Johnson and Johnson Voorsanger Productions, the game followed the titular aliens who are stuck on Earth after their spaceship crashed. One to two players had to explore procedurally generated levels to find the pieces of their spaceship. Besides the levels changing on each playthrough, the game featured items in the form of presents that could bestow good or bad effects on the player. On each play, the contents of each present box were randomly shuffled, and there was an item that would automatically reshuffle all the presents again that players could accidently activate.

Despite being inspired by earlier roguelikes, what kept *Toejam and Earl* from being referred to as one was the fact that it was played in real-time and not turn-based like the other examples. This distinction between real-time and turn-based would go on to form one of the major arguments when it comes to branding roguelikes that we will discuss in Chapter 9.

4.2 Mystery Dungeon Games

Roguelikes were a genre that began in the United States, but this did not stop other countries from making their own. One of the most popular franchises was known as the *Mystery Dungeon* games from Japan (Figure 4.2). Developed by Chunsoft,

Figure 4.2

Shiren the Wanderer would go on to have multiple entries on various platforms, but is still hard to find in the United States.

the series is made up of multiple entries featuring both original characters and licensed characters for their games. Unlike the earlier PC roguelikes, the *Mystery Dungeon* series had better art and **aesthetics**.

Two of the more recognizable entries in this series would be *Pokémon Mystery Dungeon* and *Shiren the Wanderer*. *Shiren the Wanderer* was the second official game in the *Mystery Dungeon* franchise, with its first game released in 1995 in Japan and released in the United States in 2008. Despite taking longer to come to the United States, *Shiren the Wanderer's* popularity eventually grew big enough for it to become its own series with currently five main games.

Shiren's design featured all the staples of roguelike games, but with a greater sense of persistence. During a run, players could complete bonus missions and objectives that would unlock additional features the next time they played to make things easier. There was a warehouse where players could store items that could be used in another run. Expert play was focused on leaving an item in a town where it could be upgraded once per run. Eventually, the player could take these powerful items to help them finish a run or challenge the game's optional dungeons.

Pokémon Mystery Dungeon was a spinoff of the series licensed to Chunsoft by Nintendo, with its first game released in 2005. Unlike *Shiren* and other traditional roguelikes which focused on one character, the player had a team of up to three Pokémon that they would take into the dungeons. Players always controlled one Pokémon, with the other two following the leader and being directed by the **AI**. Players were free to mix and match their party based on the Pokémon they had access to and who would help the most in the dungeon.

Shiren the Wanderer and *Pokémon Mystery Dungeon*, despite being standout examples of roguelike design, were never officially labeled or marketed as rogue-likes. The term would not achieve mainstream awareness until later.

4.3 Breath of Fire Dragon Quarter

When it comes to games being released at the wrong time, *Breath of Fire Dragon Quarter* would sadly be one of the best examples. *Dragon Quarter* debuted in 2002 as the fifth official game of the *Breath of Fire* franchise developed by Capcom. The series up until that point was a traditional **JRPG**. With *Dragon Quarter*, the developers went in a different direction.

The story followed the main character Ryu who lives in a world where humanity lives underground. His goal was to reach the surface to save the life of a woman he just met while struggling with the powers of a dragon that are slowly killing him.

Players would move around the world in real-time but would engage in tactical turn-based battles with enemies. Unlike previous games, and other JRPGs, fans were expected to play through the game multiple times. The "dragon quarter" in the title represented a ranking system featured in the game (Figure 4.3).

As players made progress, either dying and restarting or making it to the end, their rating would go up. Higher ratings would introduce additional

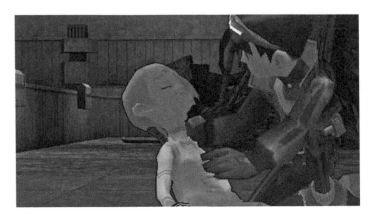

Figure 4.3

Breath of Fire Dragon Quarter was an amazing game that sadly was not what fans of JRPGs wanted to play at that time.

cutscenes to flesh out the story and unlock new areas to find better equipment. Each character could be equipped with skills learned while playing that affected their tactics during combat, and those skills would persist across plays. Getting the best rank required a near perfect run of the game, without making use of permanent saves.

There is a lot more to the design of *Dragon Quarter* that made it underrated that we do not have the space here to explore. While the game was reviewed positively, many fans and critics did not like the idea of having to restart their run to do a little better next time, with a full run of the game only taking a few hours, and *Dragon Quarter* did end up killing the *Breath of Fire* franchise.

In a way, this was the first example of **roguelite** gameplay that we will be talking in depth about in Chapter 9. The developers of *Dragon Quarter* would take their lessons learned and release the hit game *Dead Rising* in 2006. *Dead Rising* was similarly designed to allow players to carryover their unlocked abilities and stats on each run. Where *Dragon Quarter* was a turn-based RPG, *Dead Rising* was an action game with RPG stats. The series became a hit and has had four titles at the time of writing this book.

Motivating someone to restart and play through a game multiple times requires a strong design focused on replayability, and not every player has the mindset of enjoying losing progress and restarting. This became an interesting division between games that had randomized elements meant to be replayed vs. the design of roguelikes.

4.4 Randomly Generated Games

Part of the problem when it comes to labeling games as roguelikes has been the adopting of its features by other genres and designs. In the previous chapter, we discussed how ARPGs used permadeath in the form of hardcore modes. They also make use of random and procedurally generated content in the form of new equipment and the layouts of each area. Despite being set up for replayability, ARPGs are not considered true roguelikes even with permadeath.

Progression through an ARPG remains consistent in terms of story and power progression. The only unknown factor is what items will drop for a player. Modern examples tend to scale their content to the character level of the player and further limit any surprises. As we will discuss in Section 6.1, there is a lot that goes into making each play feel unique.

Roguelikes were the first genre to tout randomized content, but it has been used by many games in various ways. A popular feature in RPGs is to have a dungeon that is different each time the player enters it using procedural generation. The hit game *Bloodborne* by From Software (released in 2015) did just that with the "chalice dungeons" that players could enter to find additional rewards and fight different bosses. To be perfectly clear, permadeath and procedurally generated sections by themselves are not enough to classify a game as a roguelike.

Games that have definitive ends to them, even if they have procedurally generated areas and equipment, are not considered roguelikes. When we say "end," we are referring to a point where there is no more content or reason to keep playing. This distinction is important and something we will be discussing further in Chapter 9 as part of where the confusion over the genre comes from.

It is easy to misconstrue generating content as the "secret sauce" of good roguelike design – or simply good game design period. Without understanding the foundation of the design and gameplay potential, it is not possible to create a good roguelike. With that, it is finally time to break down the enormity of the task that goes into content generation.

5

Generating Content

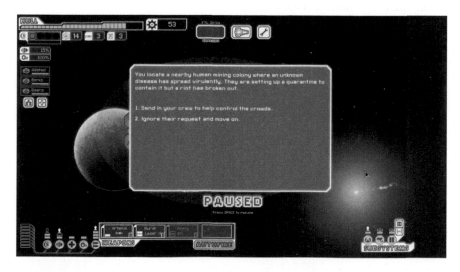

Figure 5.1

Randomizing results to actions is not as complicated as procedurally generating content, but can still impact play in large ways.

5.1 Random Generation

The act of generating content in a videogame is one of the most complicated, and oftentimes hardest, aspects when it comes to game design (Figure 5.1). There are multiple misconceptions and practices when it comes to the process and methodology of content generation that we do not have the space in this book to get into. For a more thorough examination, please read Tanya Short's *Procedural Generation in Game Design*.

We are going to be discussing the high-level philosophy of generating content, as it is a major aspect of roguelike design. Random generation is a concept that touches a wide spectrum of designs and is often confused with procedural generation.

We are going to define "random generation" as **having the game generate random results to fixed events**. Random generation is more commonly referred to as "random number generator" or **RNG** for short. When the game must decide about the outcome of an event, developers will often use RNG to make sure that the outcome is not the same each time. The implication of RNG for a design can vary between being not important all the way to game-ending, depending on how it is used.

One of the simplest examples for the consumer to understand is the concept of accuracy in RPGs. Since the beginning of the genre, designers have often created their combat systems with RNG in mind. This can be done by programming every attack to have an inherent percentage chance to hit, or using a formula based on specific attributes to determine it.

For tabletop-based games, they simply use dice rolls to determine whether something succeeds or fails. Advanced examples would change the value of the rolls based on the stats of the character or other attributes or have a chance of doing increased damage (Figure 5.2).

Figure 5.2

A randomized result means that the game is not creating new results, but simply going through a pool of possible results and deciding on what to assign.

A more complicated example of RNG is designing custom events or situations to have multiple outcomes. In Chapter 3, we discussed items having randomized effects attached to them; the effects themselves were handmade by the developer, and then the game uses RNG to decide which items they are associated with.

What is important to understand from a design point of view is that RNG does not create new results or situations in and of itself – it is merely the game choosing an outcome from a predefined list. The function of RNG is to force the player into adapting to the outcomes that occur over the course of playing. In a deck builder roguelike such as *Slay the Spire* by Mega Crit Games officially released in 2019, every card that is randomly given to the player will change how their deck behaves and makes a playthrough different.

Another interpretation of random generation is having the game just put elements in randomly without any rhyme or reason. This is something any developer should avoid doing and is a major line between good and bad roguelike design that we will look at further in this chapter. There must always be a foundation or set of rules when generating content in a game.

Given what has been said so far, the reader might assume that because RNG is not designed around having a set outcome, then it must be fair and balanced. However, that is another misconception about roguelike design and one of the hardest aspects for designers to get across to players.

5.2 Randomized Fairness

A random number generator is only about deciding the outcome of a situation; there are no feelings or emotion that comes into play. It is easy to assume that by using RNG, the developer is creating a fair experience, but fairness in the code and fairness to the player are completely different territories.

Anyone who plays games that regularly make use of RNG knows that the situation is not completely in their control. However, when RNG becomes a case of overriding the player's ability to win, it can cause players to quit in anger and frustration.

As the designer, it is up to you to make the player feel like they are the ones who are in control over whether they can succeed. The RNG of a game can feel "wrong" to the player if it seems like they do not have input into their chance of winning.

The reason for the scare quotes is that RNG can be programmed to be fair, but that by itself does not translate into a good experience. One of the most important, and hardest, lessons to get across to players when it comes to RNG is that only a 100% chance of success is guaranteed.

Anyone who has played RNG-driven games has a story about either succeeding with a low chance or failing with a high success rate. Likewise, if the player fails an 80% or up event the first time, repeating it will not guarantee a success a second time (Figure 5.3).

Figure 5.3

A good player can always prepare for RNG to some extent, but it can still feel like a slap in the face whenever something goes wrong.

Another misconception about roguelike design is that roguelikes are pure chaos – that anything and everything could happen at any time. From a design point of view, chaos is something any designer wants to avoid because it ruins any chance of creating a balanced **game space**.

In the game *Tharsis* by Choice Provisions, released in 2016, players had to use dice rolls to fix threats to their spaceship for each round of play. The threats the player had to deal with for every round were completely randomized. One player could get lucky and beat the game by only getting the mildest of events, while someone else could lose on the very first turn by no fault of their own.

The challenge of a good roguelike is to have a well-designed **progression curve** that can be tracked while still providing replayability and being mostly unpredictable.

To achieve this, designers will often metaphorically tip the scales when it comes to RNG's impact. With world or game space generation, the **algorithm** for generating the space may be set up with explicit rules to determine what areas or enemies to **spawn** around the starting position, or even something as simple as having a weapon appear within the proximity of the starting point to help give the player a fighting chance.

For games that are built on the RNG of accuracy, designers may try and "tilt" it to the player's advantage. A famous example is from *XCOM* and *XCOM 2* by Firaxis, originally released in 2012. In interviews and design talks, it was revealed that every time the player misses a shot on an enemy, the subsequent attack's chance would be 10% higher on that enemy than the game would report to the player until a hit was achieved, and then it would go back to normal.

The problem when it comes to understanding the impact of RNG is that good user interface (**UI**) design purposely hides the numbers from the players to minimize the information the player needs to know. Someone playing a game will have no idea what the difference is between a 50% and a 60% chance of landing an attack and whether that 10% mattered. The only exception to this rule is RPGs that feature "combat logs" that show the math and internal calculations to the player.

No matter how much or how little RNG there is in a roguelike, there is one golden rule regarding the player's experience that must be followed: The player needs to understand the consequences of their decisions (Figure 5.4).

The UI of the game must provide the player with enough detail so that they can plan out their next action regardless of the RNG at play. Information such as the chance to hit/miss, how much damage will be done, how much damage will the player take, and so on. Depending on the design, some of that information may be hidden, but the player still needs something. Without that information, the player will not be able to make an informed decision and will feel that they are not in control of their actions.

There are plenty of ways to build an elegant UI to display this information. One of the best examples would be *Slay the Spire*, that cleanly shows the results of each turn on both sides, and updates dynamically based on the cards played. Due to the slower nature of roguelike games, dynamic UIs work well to keep the

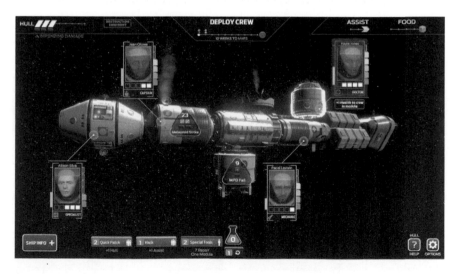

Figure 5.4

In this scene from the very first turn of Tharsis, the player is already facing a potential lose before they even begin, but they could just as well have an easy opening due to the randomness of the game.

game screen from being cluttered with detail, and only show what is relevant to the player at any given time.

A rule of thumb with UI design is that the player should not have to perform equations to figure out the outcome of decisions. Anytime the game can be direct and give the player a clear result will help the learning curve. If there is something that the player must figure out constantly, then it is considered good UI design to have the game do that calculation and show them the results.

Random generation is just part of the equation when it comes to content generation, and it is now time to talk about the other half.

5.3 Procedural Generation

Procedural generation is the cornerstone of roguelike design and one of the biggest hurdles when it comes to designing a good example. Where random generation is about picking fixed results, procedural generation is about **creating new content to change the experience on each play**.

When we use the term "new content" that is a misnomer and often a confusing point for new developers. The algorithm built by the developer goes through the content and rules defined by the developer with the algorithm and will use that when generating content.

The game is not literally building new assets, code, rules, etc., but simply mixing and matching to create the illusion of original content (Figure 5.5). For roguelikes that are organized by levels, designers will often design dozens, if not hundreds,

Figure 5.5

For this piece of gear, the primary and secondary attributes are randomly chosen during generation, while the unique set bonuses are attached to every version of the item.

5. Generating Content

of handmade individual rooms, which the game will go through when building a level to create something original each time.

Procedural generation can occur in a variety of ways, and one of the simplest examples would be the ARPG genre. To generate gear that the player can use, designers will use procedural generation and a "**loot table**" that defines all the possible modifiers for a piece of equipment and the range in terms of stats.

In games that generate the environment or game space, procedural generation is used to make sure that each playthrough takes place in a different world, but can still have set elements to it that we will be discussing in the next section. For games featuring a huge environment (or environments) to explore, it would take too much time to create all that space by hand. Instead, developers will procedurally generate the game space, and then add in handmade content and touches.

The complexity of procedural generation brings up one of the biggest misconceptions for new developers when it comes to its use: That by generating content the game is essentially building itself, making it easier to develop.

This is the complete opposite and gets at the difficulty behind procedural content. When designing a game that generates content, it is up to the developer to come up with **every possible variation** when creating the algorithm for the game to use.

Procedural generation is one of those concepts that is not black or white in terms of implementation, but there is a very wide line between good and bad versions of it. To quote the opening of *Procedural Generation in Game Design*: "Procedural generation is a powerful tool and a great way to ruin your game design."

Some developers will leave the algorithm too open – and the game will just create MC Escher-style landscapes. But if things are too strict or limited, then the procedural generation is wasted on just making similar content each time.

To demonstrate the enormity and complexity of procedural generation, I have prepared a little exercise. Imagine that you are working on a game and you are building the algorithm that will procedurally generate homes for cities and towns in your world. You have decided that the game must follow these rules:

- The home must be livable.
- No two homes can be exactly alike.
- Each home must contain the following room types: Living room, dining room, kitchen, bathroom, and bedroom.
- Each room must be fully furnished and painted.

Using pseudocode, we could try and use the following functions with "X" being a random number:

- Create Living Room (X)
- Create Dining Room (X)
- Create Kitchen (X)

- Create Bathroom (X)
- Create Bedroom (X)

Anyone who has studied programming knows the problem we have created with that code. If the game can choose any random number, we could end up with a home that has 5,323 living rooms, 20,000 dining rooms, 22 kitchens, 83,432,345 bedrooms, and 1 bathroom.

To make this work, rules need to be set up to limit the options in the algorithm:

- Create Living Room (1)
- Create Dining Room (1)
- Create Kitchen (1)
- Create Bathroom (1–4)
- Create Bedroom (1–4)

Now the game knows that there are specific limits for each room type, but there is still a problem. We cannot guarantee that the number of bathrooms will make sense with the number of bedrooms (we are a stickler for detail). Let us try this:

- Create Living Room
- Create Dining Room
- Create Kitchen
- Create Bedroom (2–4)
- Create Bathroom (Number of Bedrooms minus 1)

We are starting to create an algorithm that understands the relationship of the different elements. This is important when using procedural generation, as decisions cannot occur independently from one another.

Unfortunately, we are far from being finished. Just generating rooms does not mean anything if they are not placed within the world, and there is still the ruleset for how the rooms are connected to one another. We will be returning to this example in Section 6.3 to explore how to begin thinking about placing these elements in the world.

We have not even discussed how the game will generate the furnishings and paint for each room. For added complexity, this entire discussion has been about generating a subset of your overall game space and does not even begin to factor in how this will impact gameplay.

You may be thinking to yourself, "this sounds like a lot of work for something insignificant," and that is entirely right. Procedural generation in any title must be handled with care. It is extremely easy to create more work for yourself that will ultimately not be a factor in how someone plays your game. One key takeaway is that procedural generation is about setting up specific and detailed rules for your game to follow. From a design point of view, the game should not generate anything that has not been factored in by the developer.

There must always be a baseline or foundation for the game to use when generating content procedurally. Going back to the APRG example, developers will still have set rules for each weapon type in terms of utility and base stats that are factored in when generating them. An easy example is making sure that two-handed (or heavy) weapons have the range of their attack stat higher compared to smaller weapons to balance out the player not being able to equip a shield or some other secondary equipment in their offhand.

For world or level generation, developers will put in hard rules for what content can appear. For example, if we are building a level in a fiery environment, we should not expect to see any snowmen or ice-related challenges. If there are elements or events that are required to make progress – such as the exit to the next stage – having the game always generate them must be a part of the algorithm (Figure 5.6).

Whenever procedural generation is used, the developer is giving up some of their control of how someone experiences their game. In Section 6.5, we will talk about how balance plays a role when there is no fixed experience.

The final point for this section is a crucial one: **Procedural generation will not save a bad game**. If a handcrafted version of your game is not enjoyable, making everything procedurally generated will not make it better: It will be unfocused, and still not enjoyable. Speaking about "handcrafted," if the purpose of the game

Figure 5.6

When procedurally generating levels, there should always be major events to frame each level around.

is about telling a fixed story, or challenging the player with unique content, procedural generation will get in the way of that.

Good examples of procedural generation can still create a guided experience for the player from start to finish. However, there is no way of knowing exactly what the player has found or their overall power. Any time you have fixed content in a roguelike, that creates set elements that will occur: A boss fight, a specific challenge, and so on. The point of roguelike design and content generation is that each play should be a different experience. If an encounter is too fixed in terms of its solution, this can make the game frustrating if the player must hope that they get the solution to winning while playing.

The procedural nature of roguelikes is an important aspect of their popularity and longevity. In Section 10.1, we will look at the pacing and structure of roguelikes and take a closer look at how roguelikes differ from other genres.

Creating fixed elements is still important to having control over the experience and is the next topic for this chapter.

5.4 Explaining Points of Interest

In the previous section we talked about the idea of establishing rules that the game must abide by when generating content. Part of that means having a structure to guide the player and dictate the experience.

In the next chapter we will be discussing structure in depth, but it is important to understand the idea of having fixed content in a procedurally generated space. For lack of a better term, we will refer to these elements as **points of interest**.

Figure 5.7

A point of interest is always a fixed event within the game, but could have different outcomes such as the items in a shop.

A point of interest (or POI) is any fixed event or piece of content that can show up randomly during a play (Figure 5.7).

When it comes to designing a POI, the only limitation is the imagination of the developer. The purpose of POIs is to create a set event or situation that the player can plan for.

A simple example is generating a shop or a boss fight in each level of a game. For games that are trying to tell a story or move a narrative along, POIs are set pieces that can occur to either reveal something to the player or test them with a challenge.

Depending on the game's design, POIs can have randomness to them. With the shop and boss example, in *The Binding of Isaac* by Edmund McMillen first released in 2011, the player knows those POIs will show up on every floor, but they won't know what the shop will stock or what boss they are going to be facing. When building a roguelike, it is important to keep track of all the POIs and their function for the game.

Some developers will have a pool of POIs and during the level generation will use a random assortment of POIs to keep the player guessing. While POIs create structure to a game, it is important to make the rest of the game space interesting as well.

Some titles will generate very wide game spaces where nothing really happens, and the only content that matters is the POIs. In Section 10.3, we will discuss the concept of having an **open-world** structure and the risks and rewards that go with it.

While story POIs can have a fixed conclusion, it is often better to have multiple outcomes for a POI to prevent the game from becoming repetitive. The shop example is the easiest to understand – by changing the stock of items on each generation, it means the player knows that the shop will provide them with something, but they won't be able to know 100% what they're going to get.

A POI can either be universal and show up throughout the game or be set up to occur in specific **biomes**. Advanced design can feature a POI that is part of a chain of POIs that could happen if the player chooses an option. For example: The player is asked to decide what to do with ill-gotten money after defeating a thief; if the player keeps the money, there is the chance for an event when the police come to arrest them for keeping it.

To finish this chapter, it is important to discuss one final aspect of content generation.

5.5 Random vs. Procedural Generation?

Given what we have discussed in this chapter, someone might assume that procedural and random generation are at odds with each other, and wonder if one is clearly better than the other. The truth is any roguelike will make use of both kinds of generation (Figure 5.8).

The combination of random and procedural generation is essential to create order, while still providing a different experience. A randomly generated game space that just moves the same elements around will get boring fast, and

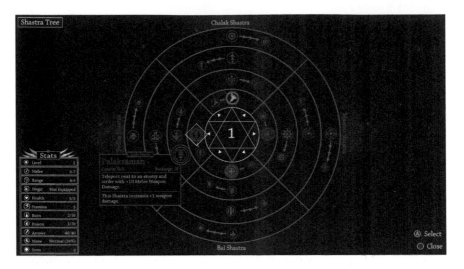

Figure 5.8

Taking fixed elements and randomizing them can lead to procedurally generated outcomes, such as this skill tree from *Asura*.

procedurally generating outcomes and rules will leave the player with little control or understanding about what is going on. There must always be a foundation for how the game will make use of random and procedural generation (procgen), and we will be discussing this more in Section 6.3.

For a better understanding of the roles both forms of content generation have, we can turn to *The Binding of Isaac* to see the difference in terms of generation. In Section 5.3, we touched on the idea of using handmade rooms that are then "stitched" together to create a new level, which *The Binding of Isaac* does. For any of the POIs that can show up, the game will randomly choose the items or outcomes from a fixed pool. In this aspect, the game has the best of both worlds: The game space is different each time, while the randomized choices keep the player on their toes.

While that may be the standard use of procgen with random generation, any aspect of a title that the designer wants to keep varied can use these systems. In the game *Asura* by Ogre Head Studios, released in 2017, the skill tree that the player picks their abilities from is procedurally generated each play. How it works is that the tree is broken down into four categories representing different styles of play. Each category has a pool of skills that the game can decide to put into the skill tree when generating the game.

Understanding what aspects of your game will be different each time you play leads into the next discussion about variance, and why not all generated content has the same impact.

6

Advanced Roguelike Design

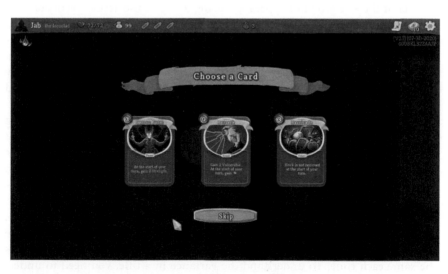

Figure 6.1

Something as simple as having the player choose their next reward can lead into constant decision-making and variance.

6.1 Creating Variance

In the previous chapter we focused on the concept of generating content and how it is essential to making a roguelike replayable. It is time to take things a step further and discuss what **variance** means, and how content generation is not enough.

Variance, defined for this book, is the ways a game can create **different and balanced playthroughs**. Replayability has become a blanket term to describe any reason to replay a title, but variance is all about how the game can make itself replayable (Figure 6.1).

Generating content is not enough to create variance, which is another misconception about roguelike design. Lesser examples of roguelikes, or just procedurally generated titles, will not go far enough with content generation. What ends up happening is that while the game is creating a new level or run, the game space itself is not changing enough to make each one feel different.

A popular genre example comes from survival games that will drop the player into a procedurally generated world and challenge them to survive. The player's ability to survive is based on gathering specific resources and using them to craft items and equipment that will aid in their survival. No matter how the game space is generated, the player must still progress through the game the same way every time – collecting the resources and crafting items in a fixed order.

For roguelikes, there may not be enough content or difference between the runs to create variance. It does not matter if the game procedurally generates all the environments in it if there are only a handful of possible outcomes. If there is no growth that can occur during play and the only progress is by beating the stage or boss, then the rest of playing the game really does not matter.

Even if there is growth happening during a run, if the actual events of each run are not different enough or push the player, then they are just repeating the game actions each time. This is often an issue seen in action-focused roguelikes that are more about the player's skill as opposed to what occurs during a run. When the player becomes so good at the game, they can make do with almost any item or luck. Fortunately, this is more of a problem at the master level of play, and most consumers will not reach that point.

With the roguelikes we are going to discuss throughout this book, playing through the levels matters because the items found can drastically change what happens in a run, and in doing so, create variance. Ultimately, variance is about forcing the player to "pivot" during their play. This could be finding a good item that changes their play, an event that shakes things up, or just the constant decision making that comes when deciding what to do next.

This is also why games that focus too much on POIs tend to become repetitive, as the player's journey is only about them and nothing else. Even if the entire game space is generated on each play, the actual path through the game remains the same each time. To understand the variance in a title, you need to understand what kind of content has been developed that the game will pull from when generating.

6.2 Categories of Content

Being able to compartmentalize and organize the type of content in your game is an essential part of making a roguelike. Each category represents a possible type of content that can appear and can be delineated further based on each listing. Here is a small example with a weapon category:

WEAPONS

1. One-Handed Weapons
    a. Sword
        i. *Stats*
    b. Knife
        i. *Stats*
2. Ranged Weapons
    a. Crossbow
        i. *Stats*
        ii. Ammo Type
    b. Pistol
        i. *Stats*
        ii. Ammo Type

When organizing your content in terms of the game space, these lists can get detailed:

BIOME

1. Fire
    a. Hazards
        i. Lava
        ii. Exploding Rocks
    b. Enemies
        i. Dragon Species
            1. Mother Dragon
            2. Baby Dragon
            3. Elder Dragon
        ii. Golem Species
            1. Rock Golem
            2. Lava Golem
            3. Fire Golem
    c. Resources
        i. Coal
        ii. Stone
        iii. Obsidian
    d. Treasure Items
        i. Magic Armor
        ii. Magic Staff

e. Points of Interest
    i. Hot Springs
        1. Player can recover health
    ii. Fire Temple
        1. Dungeon encounter
    iii. Dragon Nest
        1. Higher chance of spawning dragons and treasure chests

Each sub-listing mentioned must also be further broken down by how they work within the world. Take note of how the different categories are layered together, as this affects the variance that the game can generate.

Adding new listings to an already existing category will not create variance. With the weapon example, creating a new one-handed weapon "Mace" gives the player more options, but it is not changing how someone would play through the game. On the other hand, a new weapon category called "Magic Tome" filled with its own unique listings would.

Changing the position of a biome would also not create variance, as all the elements of the said biome are still the same. In Chapter 5, we discussed roguelikes that are focused only on POIs, and it is easy to see why they do not create variance from the biome example. A fixed event in a predefined biome will not give a different experience each time the player runs through it (Figure 6.2).

If the pool of possible options is too small, then all the procedural generation in the world will not create variance, and we could see that with the stealth

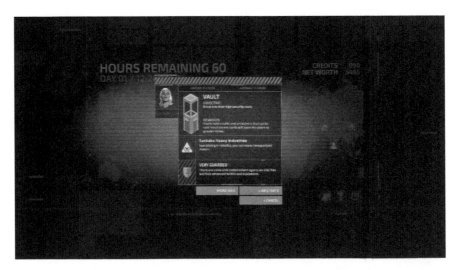

Figure 6.2

In this screen from *Invisible, Inc.* we can see the three factors that go into generating levels (the objective, the corporation, and the guard/security level), and that limited pool of options hurt the variance.

roguelike *Invisible, Inc.* by Klei Entertainment (released in 2015). Each play featured procedurally generated levels that challenged players to find all the resources, complete the objective, and then escape with their agents alive. The issue was that even though the levels the game threw at the player were procedural, the obstacles and events were limited.

There were only a handful of objective types (a fixed goal in the level) that the game would use, and there were only a few enemy factions (which determined what forces would show up). It did not take long to find the strategies that worked the best, and maps would start to feel like a chore instead of a challenge. Due to the limited ways the player interacted with world, it also reduced the variance of the game thanks to the small number of viable ways to win.

When designing a roguelike, it is important to chart how many categories of content will be in the base game. The categories themselves will be defined by the developer, and players will come to know what to expect when running through the game. Therefore, developers will often release expansions or downloadable content (**DLC**) to add more variety to their game and hopefully earn more profit. Another difference between a roguelike and traditional game is the kind of additional content that works best, and that will be discussed in Section 6.4.

Knowing what kind of content will be in a game is the first step; the next order of business is figuring out how it is placed within the world.

6.3 Structuring Your Content

No matter how much content generation there is in a roguelike, the designer must still create a structure for how the game will play. This means creating the blueprint for how the game space will look and rules to govern where and what content will appear. We will return to our house example from Section 5.3 in a minute, but it is important to discuss popular designs in roguelikes.

The longest-running and standard structure is a level/floor design. The game will either generate levels one at a time or all the levels at the start of a playthrough. The size of a level is dependent on what the designer wants. Some games could make a level a single room, multiple rooms, or a range that determines the size.

It is important when defining the algorithm to set rules in place for what can spawn on any given level – having level-20 enemies fill the first floor of a game is not a balanced experience. The blueprint for level design should not change that much across the game, but it is fair to add or remove elements to increase the difficulty as the player gets further in.

The second kind of structure is a node-based system. Instead of generating entire landscapes and stages, the game will instead focus on a series of encounters. Each node on the map is a POI, and the event can be revealed or hidden depending on the design. The player will only be able to travel from one node to the next, removing the need to explore and focus the game experience. Node travel can either be one-way or allow the player to backtrack depending on the design.

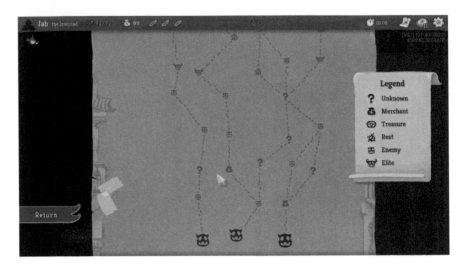

Figure 6.3

A node-based system limits the game space dramatically, but also focuses the playthrough and every choice the player makes.

The kinds of POIs remain consistent from one map to the next, but each area of the game should have specialized POIs. In the game *Slay the Spire*, a playthrough goes through three maps of nodes, with each map impacting what enemies will appear and having unique event POIs to go with it. Of the three types of structures, a node-based one is the most cost effective, as there are fewer environments that need to be designed, and a lesser need for animating characters. When it comes to balancing the design of a run, node-based has the advantage of having a fixed number of events and possible options that keep pushing the player through the run (Figure 6.3).

Lastly there is the open-world structure which creates a wide game space and fills it with POIs for the player to explore. Some titles will have the overall topography procedurally generated to frame the game space and then go in and hand-make POIs and major areas. Other roguelikes will base the world on the player's starting point and work out from there.

Biomes are often used to compartmentalize each area and try to create a diverse landscape for the player to explore. Outside of the POIs, the world itself will only provide basic gameplay interactions, which often make open-world-styled roguelikes a bit bland. We will be returning to this concept in Section 10.2, looking at games that attempted this structure.

Figuring out the structure of how content works in a roguelike is essential for creating an algorithm that defines content generation. Returning to the house example, this was where the pseudo code was at:

- Create Living Room
- Create Dining Room
- Create Kitchen
- Create Bedroom (2–4)
- Create Bathroom (Number of Bedrooms –minus 1)

This would come up with the basic structure but fails to place them in any kind of position within the world. Depending on the game's design, a stage or open-world structure would work the best. The next step would be to figure out how the algorithm creates a house. The first thing is determining where someone would enter the house.

When setting up the structure of the game, knowing where the player begins is vital, because the world or stage is built around the starting point. With the open-world structure, the algorithm will purposely generate easier biomes closer to the player's starting position and save the harder content for further out.

With the house example, the game needs to generate and place the front door, which will determine the starting point of entering the home. The game must then decide what room to connect to.

For older roguelikes, a simple solution was to have a "door" possibly spawn on any wall of a square room. Hallways would be generated to connect from one room's door to another, which often led to maze-like passageways between rooms. Modern examples that use handmade rooms will determine beforehand how big the stage needs to be, and then begin selecting, at random, what rooms will make up that level. For games that do not use a standard size for a room, the game must check to make sure that a chosen room will not conflict with the boundary of the stage or intersect with another room.

Again, it needs to be clarified that our house example is of the most basic variety; imagine designing the algorithm for a multi-floor 3D home and all the rules and coding that must be done properly. There are many ways of defining how a level is built based on the design. Even though many roguelikes will have one defined path to an exit, it is possible to procedurally generate multiple paths, or even have multiple exits.

Some developers will purposely introduce elements that do not fit within the normal rules of play. This could be the introduction of a chance of generating a higher-level piece of equipment than normal or taking a stronger enemy from later in the game and having them show up earlier. Breaking your own rules can work, but you need to understand and create said rules first.

Moving on, it is time to discuss expanding a roguelike with more content and how they differ from other videogames.

6.4 Supplemental Content

In Section 6.2, we discussed how content can be categorized to see the extent and variety your game can deliver. When it comes to growing a game and adding more content, roguelikes are different from other games. To most people, adding content to a game means adding length – a 20-hour game getting a 5-hour expansion for instance. For roguelikes, a key part of the balance of their design is having an average length per play. Directly adding length to a roguelike changes how the game is played and will require further balancing of new content and making sure that what is there can still be viable.

Even then, adding length does not impact the content that came before it, and the player will still be doing the same things for that part of the game. From a design point of view, you do not want to only add content that only changes a part of the experience and leave the rest alone. For these reasons, roguelike designers will often make use of what I have coined as **supplemental content** when expanding a roguelike (Figure 6.4).

Supplemental content grows the experience by adding more elements to the content categories, and sometimes new categories, without directly affecting the length of the game. A few examples are new biomes, new enemy types, new enemies for preexisting types, and new POIs that can show up.

If a playthrough of a game lasts about 30 minutes, supplemental content is not going to increase that length, but provide more elements that can appear in each 30-minute play. Advanced examples would include entirely new systems that can supplement playing the game, making it easier, harder, or both.

While not a roguelike, *XCOM 2* had extensive supplemental content added with its expansion: *War of the Chosen*. Besides adding to its content categories, the developers implemented new systems for how characters could grow in power,

Figure 6.4

Supplemental content can affect how someone plays a game dramatically, but does not affect the pacing or length of a playthrough.

team up during combat, and new rules for a brand-new enemy type. When done properly, supplemental content can make a great game even better and extend the market life for it. Adding in new content, supplemental or not, has become a major marketing strategy for studios. In today's market, many big-name releases also come with the promise of months, or years, of additional planned content, a notable example being Paradox Interactive who routinely support their games with supplemental content.

All this random and procedural content creates another problem – how do you balance your game?

6.5 Randomized Balance

In a standard videogame, developers know at any given time what the power level or abilities of a character and player are. This kind of set design provides a framing that can be used when balancing encounters, stages, new gear, etc.

With a roguelike, on the other hand, there is no way of knowing exactly what the player has on any given run. This is important when it comes to balancing and designing. For example, let us say that the boss on floor five attacks anything that enters its melee range, pushing it away. This fight would obviously require a range build to make progress, but what happens if the player does not have that weapon?

Enemy encounters and situations must be balanced to accommodate the kinds of strategies and options the player can get. Some options will always be better or worse for an encounter – that's just how design works – but nothing should be completely worthless (Figure 6.5).

Figure 6.5

The sheer number of items in *The Binding of Isaac* prevent any attempt at having a balanced experience, but that unpredictability also adds to the variance.

One design flaw with *Slay the Spire* was that the game allowed different kinds of builds based on the class the player chose, and what cards could show up during a run. The player did not know what encounters and bosses they were going to fight until they reached the floor and saw the map. The issue came with the boss designs. The third map pool of bosses was explicitly balanced to counter specific build strategies. The player could have a flawless run up until that point end due to the boss punishing the player for something they could not have predicted.

Beware of designing encounters that can hard counter a strategy. Any strategy or option that is not remotely viable from beginning to end is a "false choice" and punishes the player for trying to use it. Likewise, there should not be any option that is so good the player must take it or be penalized, as that would be another false choice.

The more options built into a roguelike, the greater the pool of choices that the player can get. Some developers will make use of a loot table that picks possible rewards per event or floor – providing some idea as to what the player will have access to. Another solution is to purposely keep the pool of choices on the smaller side, giving both the player and the developer a good idea of what rewards can appear during a run.

There is no such thing as perfect balance in a roguelike – that is just the nature of the genre. With *The Binding of Isaac*, when I spoke with Edmund McMillen in an online interview, he spoke about giving up on trying to completely balance the game. His reasoning was that a big part of the appeal of playing *The Binding of Isaac* was to see what combination of items could show up during a run, and he wanted things to be completely unpredictable.

An issue some developers run into is trying to chase balance in their roguelike and neutering their options as a result. The beauty of *The Binding of Isaac* came from that unpredictability of item interaction. Some runs turned into a cakewalk with an overpowered build; others could be life-or-death struggles. There are items in the game that are bad to take or just on the lower end of the power scale. The reason why it is okay here is that the player's strategy is the combination of many items, and one bad one is often not enough to sink a run.

Even with the wide degree of variance, it is still important to consider the overall balance of your options. If there is a low-cost, easy-to-perform, and easily replicable strategy that wins every time, players will become bored with the game. On the other hand, having a build that is unstoppable but requires a specific set of conditions or items to happen can be viewed as getting one over on the game.

Balance can be a never-ending challenge for developers, and it becomes harder when there are fixed elements in the game. In the game *Darkest Dungeon* by Redhook Games, released in 2016, players built 4-person teams out of a possibility of 17 different classes. Enemy party compositions were fixed – including boss fights – and meant that there were specific party combinations players could build that would have the best chance at winning. The game received multiple patches to remove easy strategies for winning, without getting rid of too many winning builds. There is more to discuss about balance in roguelike design, and we will return to this topic in Section 10.7.

Given the unpredictability of roguelike design, designers have been paying more attention to persistence as a way of giving players more chances to succeed.

6.6 Persistence Systems

Carrying over content between runs has been a part of roguelike design since the beginning, as we mentioned in Chapter 1. Modern roguelikes have been taking this carryover in a different direction and integrating it into the core gameplay (Figure 6.6).

The basic example is that by earning rewards or completing tasks in a run, the player can unlock new content that can show up in future runs or allow the player to begin with different conditions. The goal is to make the game grow the more someone plays the game and to keep the gameplay from becoming repetitive. This content is not limited to only helpful items and could include new enemies or events that can appear. In this regard, how someone can play the game changes based on the number of things that have been unlocked. In the next chapter, we will be discussing how *The Binding of Isaac* was a quintessential example of this.

For titles that are built on RPG **abstraction**, another form of persistence is providing the player with the means of permanently upgrading their character.

Figure 6.6

Incremental upgrades are a popular way of adding persistence – making the character better or the game easier to play, without having to design new content or systems.

The popular implementation uses two kinds of in-game currency: A per-run resource and a persistent one. The per-run resource is used to buy items or make use of services during a play and is often wiped with each new run (some games allow the player to carry over some of this). The persistent resource is harder to come by and is often awarded for beating bosses or accomplishing tasks. By using this resource, a player can improve their options – making future runs easier and allowing them to progress farther than before.

It is also possible to lock game systems behind the persistence – allowing players to slowly get used to the existing systems before complicating things. The risk is that the player may get bored or stop playing before that content becomes available.

An important aspect of this system, and something we will return to in Chapter 9, is the impact persistence has on balance and defining a roguelike. Traditional roguelikes do their best to keep each run as encapsulated as possible: So that the decisions and elements of one run do not start the player off better or worse in the next.

When the player can permanently upgrade their character, it means that the game is no longer being balanced on a run-by-run basis. Roguelikes that make use of persistence have a harder time in terms of figuring out how to balance their options, knowing that the player is always progressively getting stronger.

The positive of permanent upgrades is that, given time, almost every player should be able to beat the game by allowing the upgrades to compensate for skill. Some developers will put a hard cap on how much the player can upgrade the various aspects of their characters to combat this (Figure 6.7).

Figure 6.7

The longer someone plays a game with persistent elements, the more content gets unlocked and the game should get easier.

The larger problem is when designers use the persistence system as a metric when balancing the game. This means that unlike traditional roguelikes that are about mastering the rules and **mechanics**, the player may not have the ability to beat the game until they have made use of the persistence systems.

In effect, it downplays the runs where the player has no, or little, chance of winning. One of the complaints I had about *Shiren the Wanderer* was with the bonus dungeons. Unlike the main game, the bonus dungeons demanded that the player brought in their own equipment, which required multiple runs to upgrade and find the necessary gear. If the player fails the dungeon, all the gear and time spent getting them are lost. There are ways to preserve challenge while providing long-term persistence with the use of a **progressive difficulty** that will be discussed in Section 10.8.

Another option is integrating the persistence into the experience and as part of the storytelling. This can be done by restricting how far the player can improve themselves until they have made progress in the game. In the *Darkest Dungeon*, the character and equipment level ranges are between one and five. The player can only improve a character's equipment up to the same level as the character, and the player must use persistent resources to upgrade the blacksmith to do this. By upgrading the hamlet with resources, subsequent characters become easier to upgrade and maintain while allowing the player to push toward the endgame.

Ultimately the goal of persistence systems is to grow and change the experience of the game over its many runs. With that said, persistence systems are one of the major sticking points with older fans of roguelike design and a part of the argument that we will be discussing in Chapter 9.

The elements featured in this chapter took on a larger role in the 2010s and impacted how roguelike design became modernized.

7

The Roguelike Rises

Figure 7.1

Spelunky was arguably the first of the nontraditional roguelikes to not be based on RPG systems, but on platforming with its design.

7.1 *Spelunky*

In the 2010s, we saw a redesign of the term roguelike with titles that made use of permadeath and content generation but without the classic turn-based design. Originally released in 2008, and then re-released across multiple platforms in 2012, *Spelunky* is arguably one of the most recognizable roguelikes on the market (Figure 7.1).

Designed by Derek Yu, *Spelunky* challenged players to move through procedurally generated areas to reach the exit while dodging all manner of death traps standing in their way. What made *Spelunky* so unique was that gameplay was built on platforming and not the RPG structure of previous roguelikes.

This was a game in which the player's skill and their ability to control the character determined success. As a platformer, *Spelunky* was not that difficult compared to examples that came before it, but the procedural design meant that every play was different.

The structure of the procgen would always place the player in the top-left or top-right corner of the stage, with the exit somewhere on the bottom-most layer. Items could be found to make things easier, but the player was always one mistake away from dying and restarting the run. Even with health upgrades earned by rescuing people, every biome had at least one death trap that would be an instant kill if they fell into it.

Spelunky did not feature persistence in terms of unlocking new gameplay; new character models that did not affect playing it were added in the 2012 re-release. By completing objectives for a character, players could unlock shortcuts to skip over a biome, but expert players would not do this. To unlock the game's hidden and hardest biome, hell, players had to perform specific tasks and gather items in the previous biomes.

Spelunky is also limited when it comes to variance. The algorithm that defines the procedural generation is advanced, but there are not enough elements to make each run different. Each biome is strict in terms of the enemies, obstacles, and possible events that can occur. The focus on the player's ability means that once someone has got good enough to beat the game, there is not anything left for the game to throw at them. Therefore, many expert players focused on going after high scores by collecting treasure for points and making the game harder in that respect.

Spelunky's influence on roguelike design showed that designers could take the elements of a roguelike and fit them into other genres and designs, and this is why it was featured in my first book, *20 Essential Games to Study* (Taylor & Francis, 2019).

7.2 *The Binding of Isaac*

Another entry from *20 Essential Games to Study*, *The Binding of Isaac* was the first of the modern roguelikes to understand the importance of variance in terms of making a roguelike replayable. Played from a top-down viewpoint, players had

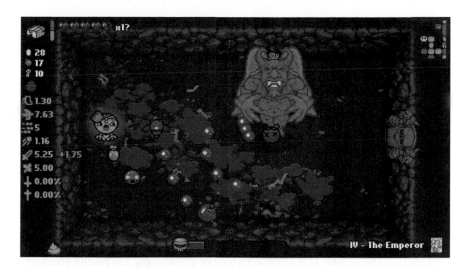

Figure 7.2

The Binding of Isaac could truly boast that no two runs were ever the same, thanks to the variance in biomes, level generation, and what items could appear during a playthrough.

to help Isaac escape the labyrinth under his house to get away from his insane mother.

As with *Spelunky*, the game's structure was focused on the biomes that dictated what rooms would be used when generating a level. The key aspect of the gameplay was the use of items that affected how Isaac behaved. On each floor there was a treasure room, and a boss fight that would drop an item (Figure 7.2).

All the named items in *The Binding of Isaac* were fixed in terms of their properties, but the game randomly decided what items would show up in any given run. Every attribute that made up Isaac could be altered by the items: Changing the character model's size, how his attacks behaved, health points, and more.

Unlike *Spelunky*, variance was a huge element of *The Binding of Isaac* – as runs lived or died based on what items would show up. Getting the right item when the player needed it could save a run, just as a bad item could ruin it at the wrong time. When I interviewed Edmund, he mentioned how he wanted players to just take every item and let the chaos ensue. Because item properties stacked, it was possible to have runs where the player would decimate every encounter with the right combination of items.

The item design was a key element to the success of the game. There are over 300 items in the latest version of it. Not every item has an effect unique to it; many feature the same or similar bonuses (mainly ones that affect character attributes).

This was an important point about *The Binding of Isaac* and where other roguelikes tend to slip up on balance.

Some developers will have a small pool of unique equipment and items, with an even smaller selection being the ones the player wants. This can turn a roguelike into a hunt for that one specific item that guarantees the run or an easy loss if the player does not get it.

While the items are ranked by players in terms of usefulness, there is no one item that will guarantee a victory. Having duplicate effects gives the player a greater chance at finding good items that will help them, while still providing the overpowered items from time-to-time. Skilled players at the game can still win even if they do not get the best items to show up during a run.

Another major aspect of *The Binding of Isaac's* success was the use of persistence to add to the game over multiple plays. Every time the player achieved a task, they would unlock something new that would appear on subsequent runs. These unlocks included new POIs, items, enemies, and unlocking harder biomes and more endings. This also provided a way of gatekeeping the harder challenges from lesser skilled players. There are multiple endings based on what paths/items the player takes, and which bosses they end up fighting.

The Binding of Isaac is one of the most successful examples of modern roguelikes thanks to the persistence and the multiple updates that came later. Since its original release, the game has seen several expansions adding more content and modes, and fans have been making mods for it. This is also a great use of supplemental content that we talked about in the previous chapter. Not only were harder biomes added to extend the length of the game for expert players, but new rooms and variations of existing biomes appeared earlier to add more variance to the game.

At the time of writing this book, there is one more official expansion set to be released for it.

7.3 Dungeons of Dredmor

A major aspect of the roguelike genre has been the constant push and pull of defining games as roguelikes, and we will be discussing it further in Chapter 9. Over the past decade there have been roguelikes that followed the classic style, just as those that were more action-focused, but one of the most successful classical takes was 2011's *Dungeons of Dredmor*.

Developed by Gaslamp Games, *Dredmor* immediately stood out from other traditional roguelikes thanks to its cartoon and lighthearted aesthetic, with many classic roguelikes still using ASCII graphics. Instead of being grim and dark, the game was more comical with a dry humor in describing the world and enemies.

In lieu of traditional RPG classes, players could become vampires, bankers, vegans, pirates, and even weirder classes, complete with their own skill tree. From a gameplay standpoint, this was a traditional roguelike through and through – We-Go turn-based design, procedurally generated floors, and a focus on finding

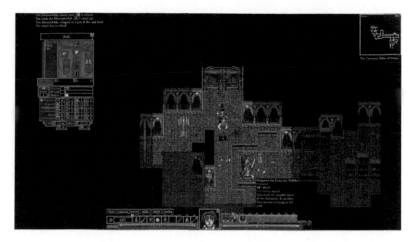

Figure 7.3

Dungeons of Dredmor played like the classic roguelikes, but was more approachable, thanks to its aesthetics and UI.

and equipping gear. Despite the lighthearted aesthetic, *Dungeons of Dredmor* was still a challenging roguelike (Figure 7.3). Figuring out what skills to take at the start was crucial, as they would define what abilities and strategies to go for during play.

As with traditional roguelikes, a lot could happen over the course of a run, from finding a random event that upgrades your weapon, to stumbling into a monster zoo (a room completely full of enemies). Players could also craft new gear if they found the required resources and recipes.

While it was not as innovative compared to the previous two games, *Dungeons of Dredmor* showed that there was still life with classic design, and more importantly, that there was always room for improvement and refinement on the formula. The focus on presentation, as much as on its gameplay, helped to make the game welcoming for new players who did not grow up on roguelikes. Having multiple difficulty levels also helped to make the game more approachable compared to its contemporaries.

The success of the games mentioned so far paved the way for a new generation of roguelikes, and the growth of the market from the indie space.

7.4 The Indie Boom

The 2010s was a decade that saw huge growth out of the indie space, and roguelikes were a major part of it. The genre became almost as popular as the platformers that indie developers focused on. Part of the reason was the success of the games we already mentioned that became the inspiration for the growing market. There are far too many games to count, but it is important to briefly mention the standout examples.

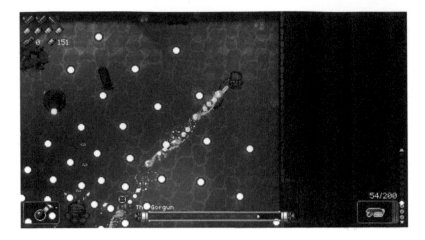

Figure 7.4

A big part of the roguelike boom was taking inspiration from other genres, particularly action-focused ones, to then apply roguelike elements to.

While not marketed or aimed at roguelike fans, the rise of the colony sim genre could also have its elements traced to roguelikes. The most famous example is *Dwarf Fortress*. The game procedurally generates the world when the player starts a new game, and their overall goal is to manage the survival of a settlement of dwarves. Permadeath for their colony meant that things could go devastatingly wrong at any time, which was part of the charm (Figure 7.4).

Faster Than Light (FTL) was not only a great roguelike but also one of the early videogame Kickstarter successes. Released in 2012 by Subset Games, the game focused on ship vs. ship combat with players having to balance power management, targeting weapons, and attending to any damage or incidents on their ship. This was also one of the first modern roguelikes to make use of a node-based system for world generation. There were not any gameplay elements that could be traced back to classic roguelikes, and we could see how the definitions of the genre began to blur.

A big part of the growing market was basing the gameplay more on action-focused titles as opposed to RPGs. *Rogue Legacy*, released in 2013 by Cellar Door Games, was an action platformer with **metroidvania**-style growth. The goal was to explore a procedurally generated castle to defeat its bosses. Each time the player died, they would be given a new ancestor who came with randomly chosen traits and classes. After each run, players spent any accumulated gold in the persistent system in the form of upgrading a castle that would unlock new passive abilities or classes that would show up in later plays. By equipping various runes, characters could perform different maneuvers like double jumping or dashing.

One of the most challenging of action-styled roguelikes was *Enter the Gungeon*, released in 2016 by Dodge Roll. Played as a top-down shooter, the goal was to complete procedurally generated floors by dodging and shooting all manner of enemies.

Like *The Binding of Isaac*, a big element of variance in a run was what items and weapons would appear. While expert players could make do with dodging and using the basic weapons, the differences between runs were like night and day.

With that said however, skill was the predominate factor in whether someone could beat the game. There is a tendency in action roguelikes to put run-critical abilities and functionality onto the items and possible rewards that can show up during play. Like *The Binding of Isaac, Enter the Gungeon* was about the mastery of the player first, and the items that appeared second.

Even light roguelike elements done properly proved to elevate titles, as demonstrated by *Darkest Dungeon*. The goal was to build teams of adventurers to explore Lovecraftian gothic dungeons to secure resources and keep parties from dying or going insane. Each map was procedurally generated with the challenge being that the player would never know exactly what horrors they would face. If a character died, they would be gone for good, and the design focused on strengthening and cultivating of surviving characters and improving the town to make things easier (Figure 7.5).

Each run into a dungeon was stressful thanks to the random events and because team members could permanently die. Unlike the other games mentioned so far,

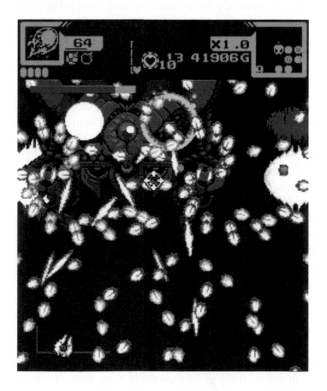

Figure 7.5

The growing trend of roguelikes in the 2010s was looking at skill-intensive games and seeing how to integrate roguelike elements into them.

Darkest Dungeon was not structured around one run per playthrough. Instead, a single play stretched out over hours of the campaign of trying to conquer the various dungeons, build teams capable of surviving, and defeat the final set of maps. Getting the pacing right in terms of playing a roguelike is difficult to do, and we will be returning to this in Section 10.1.

Making a good roguelike was enough in some cases to propel companies into stardom, and *Dead Cells*, released in 2017, did just that for studio Motion Twin. While the company had been around since 2001, it was the success of their take on roguelike design that made a name for them. The game featured a robust combat system with weapons that had their own unique properties and could be generated with special ones that could synergize off one another. The interplay between the different weapons, modifiers, and the player's own skill, proved to be an effective combination.

Dead Cells had a greater focus on the items and options that appeared over a run compared to the other roguelikes mentioned. Even though skill was a factor, the difficulty of a run could vary greatly depending on what the player found. The weapons in the game could appear at different levels of power, and the playthrough could slow down dramatically if the player did not continually find upgrades.

Over the last few years, a new design trend for roguelikes has appeared, and that is combining collectible card game (**CCG**) design to create deck builder roguelikes.

7.5 Deck-Building Roguelike Design

There is another book waiting to be written on CCG design, as it has had a fascinating history and unique design elements. When it comes to videogames, CCGs have been done as either virtual versions of existing games like Wizards of the Coast's *Magic the Gathering* (first released in 1993), or original games – such as Blizzard's *Hearthstone* (first released in 2014) – with the goal of creating a competitive and profitable title.

The idea of combining the strategic building of decks with the procedural and randomized play of roguelikes may sound strange, but it has proven to be a "chocolate and peanut butter" kind of design.

One of the first games that showed the potential for this design was *Dream Quest*, released in 2014 by Peter Whalen. *Dream Quest* is viewed by many as the progenitor for deck-building roguelikes. The gameplay loop was designed around exploring procedurally generated dungeons, but instead of finding gear, the player found new cards that could be used to attack, defend, and more during combat. Unlike the other games we are going to discuss, *Dream Quest* was focused more on the roguelike gameplay compared to the CCG.

Unlike later examples that used different formats for stage generation, *Dream Quest* went with procedurally generating every floor as traditional roguelikes did. There was no way to strategically build a synergized deck, and the limited card pool for each class did not help matters. The game did feature persistence with new classes and passive perks that would become available the better the player did (Figure 7.6).

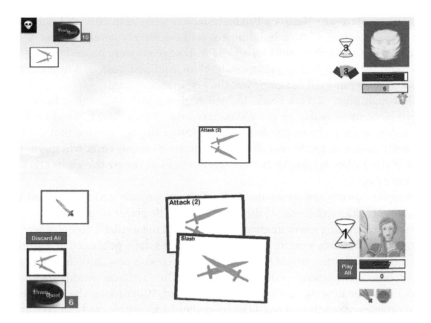

Figure 7.6

Dream Quest might lack the aesthetic of later deck builders, but its design of combining roguelike and deck builders was the start of this trend.

For an almost literal example of this combination, there was the *Hand of Fate* series, first released in 2015 by Defiant Development. Here, the player had to explore dungeons that were represented by cards on a table. The player chose a deck of cards that represented POIs and gear that they wanted to see appear in a run, while the AI – or dungeon master – shuffled its own cards in to create a run.

Battles took place in a 3D arena with the player's character using all the equipment cards they had to fight off enemies as well as bosses. The sequel expanded on the card-designed dungeons with having different stories and scenarios for the player to conquer.

Besides completing dungeons to unlock more challenges, a major form of persistence was putting in event cards in the player's deck that they wanted to complete. By solving the event, new cards would become available that could be added to the player's deck on future runs. These new cards could be better equipment or beneficial events the player could guarantee showup in the middle of a play. Unlike the other deck builders, both *Hand of Fate* games were designed around a campaign progression, with the final challenge being a dungeon where the player fought the villain responsible for the card game.

Other examples of this design tried to keep the RNG fair for players, but *Hand of Fate* often came down to luck. Winning events required the player to make a blind pick to grab a winning card from a shuffled hand. Advanced events sometimes required the player to guess correctly multiple times; messing up once would cause it to end in failure.

Monster Slayers by Nerdook Productions was released in 2017 and established the basic template of deck-building roguelikes. Players would choose a class which would affect their abilities and deck. Dungeons were procedurally generated, and the player had to explore to level up, find new gear, and upgrade their cards. A huge aspect of the game was the persistence systems.

Through play, players could unlock higher ranks that could be used to apply permanent **buffs** to the characters and classes. Gear could be found randomly at shops or in chests that went into a storage system that could be used for future runs. It was difficult to have winning runs when someone first started playing due to the stat differences between the characters and the enemies.

Slay the Spire is the game that solidified and popularized the current deck builder roguelike archetype. At the start of a run, the player would choose a class, with each class being a unique character with cards not available to the others. The game featured a node system, with the paths procedurally generated at startup.

Completing battles would allow the player to choose new cards to add to their decks, once again determined by their class. Finding artifacts would provide new buffs or change how the rules of the game worked. Win or lose, the player would earn experience points that would go toward unlocking new cards for the respective class that could show up in future runs.

Slay the Spire also introduced the concept of progressive difficulty in the form of its ascension mode that provided further challenges for players to overcome. We will return to this topic in Section 10.8.

Deck-building roguelikes are an interesting middle ground between the classical and action-focused designs. One of the reasons for their popularity and depth comes from where the focus on variance is (Figure 7.7).

Figure 7.7

Slay the Spire's design, combined with an amazing UI, made it a breakout hit among indie games and the standard for deck building roguelikes.

From a design standpoint, the level structure and enemy battles remain consistent across plays. The X factor that players must adapt to is what cards will constitute their deck in any given run. Like CCGs, high-level play is figuring out the potential of the cards that the player has at hand. A successful run is never about just one card, but the combination of different mechanics and rules coming together to create a winning strategy.

Each class has a variety of cards associated with it, and they can be further delineated into different builds for that class. In *Slay the Spire*, the ironclad class (which is the warrior archetype) has cards that favor a block-heavy style, boosting its damage, and purposely taking damage to activate a secondary effect. The player must decide what kind of strategy to focus on, while still adapting to the artifacts and events that pop up.

Unlike other roguelikes where the player has little choice in what appears during a run, deck builders are fairer in this aspect thanks to the player choosing what rewards they get from a small selection. Since the game is built on cards instead of generating items, there is a fixed pool of possibilities that the game will choose from. A typical decision that players must decide on when picking cards is to take a good card that does not work with the build they have going or focus on a leaner – but more situational – style deck. There is a feeling of satisfaction that comes with mastering the mechanics and coming up with game-winning strategies.

It is not about what the game throws at the player that gives deck-building roguelikes replayability, but what options the player can use that can vastly affect how a run plays out. Just like some of the other roguelikes we have talked about in this book, it is possible to get borderline game-breaking decks going under the right circumstances and events. Some deck builders allow the player to upgrade cards – increasing what they can do or adding new utility to them – which further provides choices to make.

The success of *Slay the Spire* has inspired multiple deck-building roguelikes that are either in early access at the time of writing this book or just released, such as 2020's *Monster Train* by Shiny Shoe. In a strange way, deck-building roguelikes are coming into their own popularity and growth, much like the action-focused ones that occurred earlier in the 2010s.

Deck-building roguelikes are just one of the examples of this "stretching" out the design of the traditional roguelike. With so many new fans and roguelike examples, the last decade saw the changing of the definition of a roguelike and the market.

7.6 Defining a Roguelike

The term roguelike has gone on to mean different things depending on what games people grew up playing (Figure 7.8).

For the market today and newer consumers, roguelikes have been defined as any game that is designed around repeated plays in a shuffled or procedurally generated space. The requirement of having RPG or turn-based design is

Figure 7.8

By the end of the 2010s, the roguelike market was completely unrecognizable compared to the past 40 years.

no longer part of the equation for these consumers and developers. We will be returning to this point in Chapter 9 to discuss the argument over the definition.

The roguelike genre has grown thanks to this easing up on the genre conventions. The common element of all the games mentioned in this chapter has been moving away from the roguelikes of the 1980s and 1990s. Even *Dungeons of Dredmor*, which is the closest to classic roguelikes, did feature differences in the aesthetics and user experience (**UX**) design, making it easier for new players to get into.

A roguelike does not mean extreme difficulty anymore, and this can be seen via difficulty levels or just simply designing an easy roguelike. Developers learned just how much value replayability and variance could add to games. In effect, this became part of the advantage that indie developers have over AAA studios.

An indie developer can make a highly focused title built on a small gameplay loop, compared to the big-budget grandiosity of AAA studios. Taking that smaller loop, it is easier to create variance and make that gameplay replayable. For AAA games that are not open world, a typical playtime can be eight to ten hours; for a well-designed roguelike, a consumer could get dozens or even hundreds of hours out of the experience. Getting that amount of play out of a roguelike is about understanding the pacing that goes into playing one, which we will be discussing in Section 10.2

Like platformers, indie developers have been exploring all aspects of what could be considered a roguelike. This variety has been the reason why the roguelike genre is now one of my favorites to play. At the same time the indie space was experimenting, a surprise game would launch the closest the AAA market has come to creating its own roguelike and invent a new subgenre as well.

8

AAA Roguelikes

Figure 8.1

Demon's Souls and the *Dark Souls* series ushered in a new era of challenging "soulslikes."

8.1 *Demon's Souls*

Demon's Souls by From Software released in 2009 was a turning point for the game industry and for the studio. Built off their previous game series *King's Field* (first released in 1994), *Demon's Souls* was an action RPG where players explored massive environments, dodging traps and fighting monsters (Figure 8.1).

The game's mantra of "Tough, but fair" could be seen throughout its gameplay loop. Combat was real-time with a huge emphasis on positioning and managing stamina. The player could not just mash the attack button and expect to win. The game buffered button inputs – meaning it would queue up the next command the player pressed while the animation they were in was still going. Paying attention to dodging or blocking attacks became essential when it came to the many fights.

Unlike other action-driven games where basic enemies were fodder for the player, this was a world where every enemy could be a threat to the unprepared. The combat system allows the player to focus on an enemy to keep the camera locked on them, but the player is not meant to fight multiple enemies at once. *Demon's Souls* brought a level of complexity to combat by slowing down combat compared to more action-oriented titles.

Players had to constantly manage stamina that allowed them to block, attack, run, or dodge enemies. Each weapon behaved differently: From quick stabs of a dagger to the slower wind up and swing of a two-handed sword (Figure 8.2).

What truly separated *Demon's Souls* from other AAA games at the time was the unique take on punishment. Players were going to die … a lot, and there was no need to have a lives system. When the player failed, their collected "souls," which acted as both experience and money, would fall to the ground where they

Figure 8.2

Soulslikes do feature character progression, but they are first and foremost about player skill.

died. Each time the player left a stage, either by dying or by returning to the hub area, all the enemies respawned and would stalk the corridors again.

One of the most stressful events in playing *Demon's Souls* was having a huge amount of souls collected and having to decide whether to retreat to safety or push on and hope to find a shortcut back to the start.

The focus on challenge and difficulty was a watershed moment for AAA developers. Up until that point, difficulty was being downplayed by major studios as there was a consensus that the player base did not want to be challenged like that. *Demon's Souls* proved that there was a viable market for harder titles.

There is a lot more to the success and design of *Demon's Souls* that I went into detail about in *20 Essential Games to Study* (Taylor & Francis, 2019), but that would not be related to the topic at hand. The success of *Demon's Souls* gave us the more recognized spin-off *Dark Souls* (first released in 2011) that elevated the gameplay further.

Dark Souls would go on to be the most successful franchise From Software made and popularized a new subgenre for roguelike design.

8.2 "Soulslike" Design

When it comes to the game industry, developers tend to be inspired and build new games from popular franchises and designs. We saw this with the rise of the open-world genre after *Grand Theft Auto 3* by Rockstar Games (released in 2001) and the 3D platformer after *Super Mario 64* (released in 1996) by Nintendo, as a few examples.

The success of *Dark Souls* coined a new genre: "**Soulslike**," to describe games that were based on the *Souls'* formula. Despite the obvious connection to a roguelike, soulslikes only focus on specific parts of the design.

Unlike roguelikes that make use of procedural generation for designing content, soulslikes take place in handmade worlds. One of the areas where the *Dark Souls* series is praised the most is with their challenging and uniquely designed worlds. Every aspect of the design of the worlds was crafted with nothing left up to chance.

As mentioned in the last section, death will reset the areas in terms of enemies and drop the player's resources on the ground. If the player dies a second time before acquiring their resources, they are permanently lost. Some soulslikes will let the player keep the resources to not overly punish the player.

The pacing and progression of a soulslike are not the same as those of the roguelike genre. Most roguelikes are designed around individual runs taking anywhere from 30 minutes to an hour to complete. A soulslike is played over multiple hours until the player reaches the final challenge and wins.

With the exception of the original *Demon's Souls*, soulslikes are built around an open-world design. The "levels" are environments with their own self-contained enemies, obstacles, and bosses. Instead of designing a level as a continued path from beginning to end, soulslikes feature more compacted design. Many paths in a level will connect to an earlier area to provide a shortcut that the player can open. Once opened, these shortcuts remain open no matter how many times the player dies (Figure 8.3).

Figure 8.3

Soulslikes tend to hit the same notes in terms of design and presentation, but no one has managed to outdo From Software yet.

There is a sense of architecture and environmental design to a good soulslike. The design is not about building mazes but attempting to combine a plausible environment with challenging level design. This focus on detail makes it easier for the player to create a mental roadmap and find their way around without the need for an in-game map.

Persistence was tied entirely to the player's character and would not reset if they died. Soulslikes typically have their version of the "souls" in the *Dark Souls* series that acts as money and experience. By spending them on their character, players would permanently improve their attributes.

By raising their attributes, characters could have more health, stamina for attacking, or allow them to wield stronger weapons. To limit this, designers will often put soft caps on the impact of their attributes. Each time the player goes to level up, they can see what areas of their character will be improved by raising specific attributes. At certain point thresholds, continuing to raise an attribute will either not improve the character, or the impact will be severely lessened.

The persistence can also be seen in the equipment found, as many soulslikes allow the player to raise the attributes on their weapons and armor. Improving the damage of a weapon provides the most noticeable improvement to the difficulty of combat. This is an important aspect of how character designs work differently compared to other RPG-based systems. Most RPGs limit the options a character can use based on their class – a warrior cannot use a mage's spells for instance.

In a soulslike, the only limitation comes from whatever stat requirements are attached to the equipment. A patient player could teach their warrior how to use magic or whatever combination they wanted.

From Software also popularized a sort of "hands-off" approach to storytelling that other developers have been chasing. The *Dark Souls* series has extensive lore and backstory about how the world came to be and the people in it but never stops the game to explain any of it. Instead, the player can choose to explore this via the lore entries on items and gear.

We have seen both 2D and 3D titles make use of all these aspects, such as *Salt and Sanctuary* by Ska Studios (released in 2016) or *The Surge* series by Deck 13 (first released in 2017), and the term "soulslike" has been attached to games almost as often as roguelikes.

With that said, soulslikes would not be considered examples of roguelikes no matter how challenging they are. A soulslike is not built around replayability or variance due to the world not being procedurally generated. While someone can replay the game with a different build, this is not the same as the game providing new or different challenges during a run.

There is one AAA game, at this time, that has managed to come the closest to roguelike design.

8.3 *Prey Mooncrash*

Prey Mooncrash is the expansion to Arkane Studios' *Prey* released in 2017. *Prey* itself was a first-person shooter built on exploring a station and **emergent gameplay** as players could solve the challenges and fight any way they wanted to.

Mooncrash took that design and condensed it down further (Figure 8.4). The concept was that the player must explore a simulation of a moonbase under attack

Figure 8.4

Unlike the soulslikes, *Prey Mooncrash* featured a set world with random events and had some of the variance we often see in roguelikes.

by the game's alien force known as the typhon. After choosing a character, the player must complete objectives and find a way to escape the moonbase.

There are multiple ways to escape with the necessary equipment randomly placed each time the player runs the simulation. The plot is that the player is trying to fix the simulation by completing objectives to figure out what truly happened.

The further the player gets in terms of their goal, the harder the simulation itself becomes. Eventually, the player will have to deal with random environmental hazards, hunt down power generators, and deal with more dangerous enemies. During play, enemies become stronger the longer the player stays alive, forcing them to move fast.

Persistence comes into play by being able to upgrade characters by finding neuromods within the world. Players can also spend points earned while playing to start with better equipment and resources to make future runs easier. By the time the player reaches the final goals of the simulation, it is possible to take a fully upgraded character and buy all the items they need to trivialize the difficulty.

Even though the world itself was not truly procedurally generated, by changing the conditions on each play, *Prey Mooncrash* does provide variance. Each area of the moonbase had specific events and items that could show up, along with fixed rooms with guaranteed supplies on each run. On later runs, one or more of the areas could suffer from a power loss, requiring the player to return to the central hub to switch battery supplies.

Prey Mooncrash is the closest at the time of writing this book that a AAA title has come to having roguelike elements, but it is not a true roguelike. With so many takes on the genre, the term has become muddled and has led to confusion among consumers and developers about how to classify games with it.

9

The Roguelike Confusion

Figure 9.1

Traditional roguelikes have not gone away, and there are still indie developers iterating on the design.

9.1 The Roguelike Debate

The history of the roguelike genre and its growth is different from other genres in the industry. Traditionally, genre definitions remained consistent, even with the growing technology and switch to 3D. A genre like platformer, first-person shooter, or RPG can still trace its design and implementation back to the origins of it (Figure 9.1).

For roguelikes, the genre has shifted as more games were released and newer developers took the reins. In Chapter 7, we looked at games that had little in common, design-wise, with older examples of the genre. This is due to developers experimenting with adding roguelike elements to other genres. The integration of action-based designs with roguelike elements over the 2010s was a major turning point for the genre.

What is important to note is that the older examples of roguelike games are not gone; there are still developers releasing games like that to this day, but they do not receive anywhere near the same coverage as the newer takes. One example would be the open-world styled roguelike *Caves of Qud* by Freehold Games (available for purchase since 2015, but still in development at this time). There are several possible reasons for this. Classic roguelike design does not often catch the eye of consumers compared to aesthetically unique games like *Dead Cells* or *FTL*. The learning curve for classic roguelikes is higher, and they are often harder to play, compared to modernized takes.

For fans who grew up with roguelikes, they do not consider any of the games mentioned in Chapter 7 (with the exception of *Dungeons of Dredmor*) as actual roguelikes. For them, a roguelike is only a title that has turn-based design, permadeath, and a focus on individual runs. And this argument has led to yet another term that is a part of this genre.

9.2 Roguelite vs. Roguelike

We have used several genre definitions in this book so far, rogue, roguelike, soulslike, but there is one that has become a point of contention in the genre and its philosophy: Roguelite.

When arguments come up over whether a game could be defined as a roguelike, people will often refer to titles as roguelites. To the reader, this may sound like a semantics issue, but there are major points of design philosophy present.

A roguelite is a title that makes use of procedural and randomized content generation but is structured around a fixed endpoint instead of a run-by-run design. Roguelikes do have a final challenge for the player to overcome, but their design is flexible enough with the procedural generation that someone can replay it and get different experiences.

Roguelites are limited in this aspect for two reasons. The scope of a roguelite is smaller compared to roguelikes, and they do not have the same level of variance built in. Even though the world is procedurally generated on each run, there are not enough elements within the design to create variance (Figure 9.2).

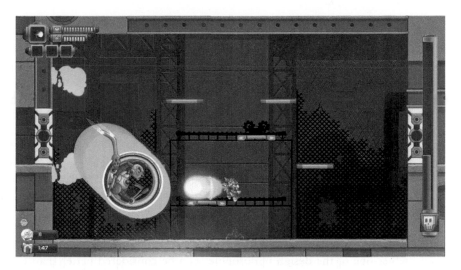

Figure 9.2

The use of persistent systems and the limited content generation limit the replay value of roguelites.

Going back to *Rogue Legacy*, the game space is centered around four biomes. Each time the player starts a run, what they are doing is not changing, but simply shuffling around elements. There are no random events or variables that change the experience, and the player's character is fixed the second they start the run.

Back in Section 6.6, we discussed the concept of persistence systems and how they create carryover from one run to the next. Roguelites are designed around the persistence constantly improving the player's character instead of having vastly different runs. With enough persistence upgrades, the player will not have to worry about anything being challenging due to the vast differences in stats.

Often in roguelites, the heavy use of persistence creates throwaway runs – where the only mission is to acquire enough resources to unlock a major upgrade to prepare for the run that matters.

Instead of the gameplay being about the runs, the focus is on a campaign-like structure or progression. Some roguelites require the player to beat a set of bosses or complete tasks to win, but they do not have to be done in a single run.

Roguelites adopt the gameplay structure of runs, but the runs are tied to finishing the game by beating the final challenge. Once the player has won, the roguelite is finished, unless the player wants to restart with a fresh save file. There are ways of adding more challenge to a game via progressive difficulty, which we will be discussing in Section 10.8.

It is possible to design either a roguelike or roguelite to be played both ways. Some titles will allow the player to turn off the persistent systems to make each run clean or turn on persistence to make things easier. For titles that have permadeath, even that can be turned on and off depending on the design.

Going back to *The Binding of Isaac*, even though persistence was a huge factor in its gameplay, the persistence itself was there to unlock more content, not provide carryover from one run to the next.

For narrative-focused titles that want to make use of procedural generation while telling a story, roguelite design is the better fit. Persistent systems can be integrated into the story and make it far more likely that players will be able to see it through to the very end. An example would be *Children of Morta* by Dead Mage (released in 2019). The game followed a family of adventurers trying to save their world. New family members and upgrades were unlocked as the player progressed through the biomes (Figure 9.3).

When marketing a title, it is important to consider what type of roguelike elements will be in your game to avoid any unnecessary confusion among fans.

As with our discussion on whether random or procedural generation is superior, neither one of the design philosophies can be considered better than the other; it always comes down to implementation.

There are examples of bad roguelikes where the player has little control over success, just as there are bad roguelites that require too much investment before the player has a chance at winning.

While this argument focuses on roguelike and roguelite terminology, there is *yet* another term that has become an alternative.

Figure 9.3

Many people feel like roguelike and roguelite can be used interchangeably to describe a game, but that is not the case from a design perspective.

9.3 Action Roguelike

The argument over roguelike and roguelite design is about the ends of the spectrum when it comes to this kind of philosophy. As we talked about in Chapter 7 however, there are games that do not fit into either grouping – a title that is not about turn-based gameplay but based around variance between runs and replayability.

Titles like *The Binding of Isaac* and *Spelunky* are focused on runs like roguelikes, but do not have the same genre qualifiers as older roguelikes. Because of this, consumers have been using the term **action roguelike** for games that do not easily fit either term.

Unlike traditional roguelikes that are about character and RPG abstraction, action roguelikes put the player's skill first and foremost. Even if the game generates equipment or allows for character progression, the player's own ability and hand-eye coordination matter the most.

In *Enter the Gungeon*, a skilled player can still pull out a win if they get bad luck with item drops, just as a lesser skilled player can lose with the best weapons in the game. Action roguelike design has created an interesting **dynamic** in how persistent systems can impact a play (Figure 9.4).

The more skilled the player is at the game, the less they need to rely on persistent upgrades and carryover. This is part of the reason why these systems are so popular today – as they provide as much or as little help without stopping

Figure 9.4

A popular option to help with difficulty is to have multiple endings/paths of varying levels of challenge. A regular player can still beat the game, while having harder areas for players to test their mastery with.

one group from enjoying the game. Persistent upgrades are often seen in action roguelikes but are not required as with the case of *The Binding of Isaac* and *Enter the Gungeon*. Making sure that the player has the tools they need to win is an important part of balance and pacing that we will come back to in Section 10.1.

The challenge of designing an action roguelike comes down to how much skill should be required to win vs. finding good items and upgrades during play. With the embrace of action elements, many action roguelikes demand quick reflexes from the player. The right items in the hands of expert players can lead to the game becoming easy for them but become required by lesser-skilled players. Changes to the balance of the game will affect all players and must be handled with care. Even though persistent systems do help, if a player feels like the game is dragging on for too long to get the necessary upgrades, they may quit out of frustration.

Action roguelikes present yet another aspect of the roguelike genre, and we already covered the other take with deck-building roguelikes in Section 7.5. With everything said, I want to provide my thoughts on this debate.

9.4 The Shades of a Rogue

When I first started to think about writing this book, it began when I saw people incorrectly label the design aspects of roguelikes and the argument of what a roguelike is that made up this chapter.

I mentioned at the beginning of this book that I did not get into the genre until the late 2000s, which colors my perspective. For many of you reading this book right now, you may have started playing them around that same time with the games discussed in Chapter 7. It is easy to assume that the first game you play is indicative of the genre, regardless of the quality of the game.

Originally my thoughts were that the old way of designing roguelikes was no longer in fashion and that the action roguelikes and roguelites had inherited the term, kind of like the evolution and growth of cars. However, that is not a fair statement – there are still turn-based/traditional roguelikes being made and a healthy market of fans for said games. There might be new elements or improvements to the UI/UX (such as the discussed *Dungeons of Dredmor*), but they are still built from the same design conventions as titles like *Nethack*. For traditional fans, there is this feeling that the genre they grew up with has been upended by newer games and people coming in over the past decade.

This is not a case of quality; as we have talked about over this book, there are amazing examples of games that have taken roguelike elements in a new direction. However, no matter how great they are, or the amount of praise mainstream consumers gave them, they do not have the same design qualifiers of the traditional roguelikes. Some say that there are only two terms, roguelikes and roguelites, but I would argue that is being too reductive of the design. Part of the reason why there is trouble classifying games within the genre is that there are too many different design philosophies to fit just one or two terms.

We could see something similar to the platformer genre that I talked about in *Game Design Deep Dive: Platformers*. From the outside it is easy to think that every platformer is like *Mario*, or every game that features jumping would be considered part of the genre. But as we discussed, the genre can be broken down into subgenres based on the design, such as adventure platformers, platformers driven by realistic physics, and others (Figure 9.5).

And that is why I feel with the roguelike genre that it has become diverse enough to support multiple subgenres. The games that emulate or build from the classics should be branded as roguelikes or "traditional roguelikes." Even if a title is designed with the same philosophy, if it does not play like those classic games, then it should not be labeled as just a roguelike, and there is nothing wrong with that.

Calling a game an action roguelike, deck-building roguelike, or a roguelite is not insulting the game or the developers. Clearer definitions of the genre will help consumers and fans know what to expect when purchasing a game. For developers, they can better market and conceptualize their designs.

The genre has grown so much over the last decade with different takes on it that no one could have foreseen back in the 1980s. Almost every genre could be

Figure 9.5

The variety of games with roguelike elements that are not traditionally design have grown enough to deserve its own genre designation.

adjusted to have roguelike or roguelite aspects to it. Part of the growth of the action roguelike category has been first-person shooters combined with the procedural design of a roguelike, and even bullet-hell shooters mixed with roguelike elements. Where the developers focus their procgen can lead to dramatically different takes on the design, even with the subgenres that we have discussed. It will be interesting to see what new takes will appear over this decade.

For the remainder of this book, the term "roguelike" will be used when we are discussing generalized aspects of the genre, and we will use the other terminology for specific design elements.

Expert Roguelike Design

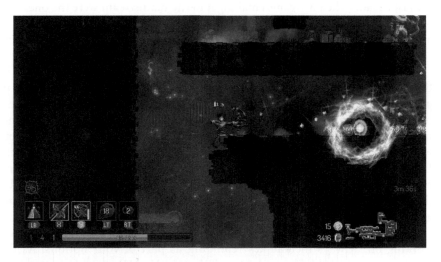

Figure 10.1

No matter what kind of roguelike you are designing, getting the basic feel and moment-to-moment gameplay right is a crucial foundation to build on. *Dead Cells* handled great from its very first early access build, and only got better from there.

10.1 Getting the Basics Right

For the final design chapter, there are still elements to discuss regardless of what kind of roguelike you may be interested in building (Figure 10.1).

Back in Section 5.3, we discussed content generation and how it will never save a bad game. Making sure that the basics of your game feel good in the player's hands is an important aspect of UI/UX design.

In the previous chapter we drew a line in the sand regarding the definitions of a roguelike and the different subgenres. With that said, just because you are designing an actual roguelike does not mean that the basic steps are done for you. This is another misconception that also relates to the platformer genre: That just because it has been around for so long, it is easy to build a good one. Good platformers, like good roguelikes, need to have a solid core gameplay loop to build from, or nothing else will matter. Even though a roguelike's design philosophy is fixed, this does not end the work in terms of the game feel. Aspects like an easy-to-understand UI and **GUI** and a good tutorial with **onboarding** are important.

One of the reasons why many roguelikes do not break through to the mainstream is the fact that little has been done in terms of **approachability** and onboarding. They are aimed at people who are already well acquainted with the genre but have little to teach new players about the design and gameplay. Even traditional roguelikes being released or developed in today's market will use the same confusing (to outsiders) UI as the games from back in the day. Something that seems universal to other genres, like gamepad support, may not be considered part of the first retail version of the game.

And that is a major part of why the genre's definition became so muddled over the last decade. The only games making it to the mainstream were the ones that focused on approachability with their design and UI. At this point, it is easy to assume that titles like *FTL*, *Dead Cells*, or *Slay the Spire* are more recognizable compared to *Rogue*, *Nethack*, and other roguelikes.

For action roguelikes specifically, they do not have the luxury of being set in their design. As a developer, you must make sure that your game feels good to play, and that requires playtesting and iteration. Just as procgen will not save a bad game, if your title does not feel good in the player's hands from minute one, that will drive away people regardless of everything else. A major aspect I note when trying out new roguelikes, or any game in general, is how the controls and UI feel at the start. Many of the standout examples of action and deck-building roguelikes mentioned in this book had great UI design. Having a dynamic UI that updates the player after every choice made helps a lot when learning any game.

A special point that needs to be mentioned, no matter what genre you are working on: Always include key rebinding as part of your options. As the developer, you should do your best to design the best UI possible, but a major point of accessibility is allowing people to make the controls feel comfortable to them.

Figure 10.2

Action roguelikes like *Enter the Gungeon* would not have been as successful if the shooting and dodging mechanics did not feel good to use.

Depending on the genre that you are building your game around, you must look at good examples of how that genre handles UI design and use that for your game. Part of the success of *Spelunky* and *Dead Cells* was that if you took away the roguelike elements, these games still handled amazingly well and were enjoyable to play.

Part of that handling has to do with the basic options or mechanics the player has access to. There is a common form of progression in games with abstracted elements to unlock ways to make the gameplay better. *Dead Cell's* metroidvania aspects are a good example, as the player can unlock the ability to wall run, making it easier to traverse the levels (Figure 10.2).

However, you do not want the game to feel sluggish or bad to play at the start of a run. This requires an understanding of the core moveset for your character. As an example, let us imagine an action roguelike that is about finding weapons to fight enemies with. At the start of a run, the player's only weapon is a knife that is slow, short-ranged, and extremely hard to use effectively. When the player gets a new weapon, the game becomes a lot more enjoyable, but restarting a run requires them to go back to the knife. Good game design is about making the basics feel great and growing things from there, not creating problems and then adding the solution later.

There is more to UI/UX design that goes beyond the genre that we do not have space here to get into. The easiest way to do the research yourself is to play both good and bad examples of the genre you are interested in – whether that is a roguelike directly, genres to add roguelike elements to, or any genre you want to build a game around. Look at what does and does not work, and anytime you feel frustrated with the game, make a mental note to avoid that with your title.

10.2 Proper Pacing

Throughout this book we have discussed how roguelikes are different from other genres in terms of design and the general playthrough. Back in Sections 6.3 and 6.4 we went over how content is structured and added to a roguelike.

When designing the overall scope of a roguelike, it is important to understand how variance and the replayable nature impact the pacing. A good roguelike is balanced around how individual runs play out, as opposed to a lengthy campaign. The longer a roguelike run is, the more "weight" gets associated with it. The amount of weight also represents the investment that goes into restarting a run. For older roguelikes like *Rogue* and *Nethack*, a single completed run could take several hours.

If the investment is too high, fans may not want to replay the game after losing all that time. However, there are fans who like lengthy roguelikes, and even if they do not immediately replay the game, they could return to it later (Figure 10.3).

Darkest Dungeon faced some criticism when it was released in terms of the penalty of failure and length of the campaign. The final dungeon required fully leveled teams built specifically to counter each stage's enemies and situations. If the player failed, they would have to repeat the leveling process with another four characters before they could try it again. The complaints led to the developers

Figure 10.3

Every aspect of your game must be balanced around the average length of a run. With *Monster Train*, the player must fight eight battles to win, and the power of their cards and enemy units are set around that.

releasing difficulty settings that affected the campaign length in terms of enemy strength and more.

Even if a roguelike has permadeath, there must still be the option to create a save to allow players to return to the game at a later point. This can also take the form of a "temporary save": Where the game saves the state of the game at that moment in time while exiting and is deleted when the player returns to the game. Some modern roguelikes make use of a lives system with their permadeath to give players multiple chances, but when they run out their character is gone.

When playing action roguelikes like *The Binding of Isaac* and *Enter the Gungeon*, a typical full run usually stays at or below an hour of play. As we mentioned earlier, each hour of playing a roguelike is a different experience thanks to the variance of content generation. With enough content, a roguelike can provide many unique hours of individualized runs. Figuring out what the average length of a run looks like is an important early step when designing any roguelike.

A point that we will be coming back to in Section 10.7 is that even with variance, there is no such thing as an infinitely replayable roguelike without having additional content added in.

The number of unique biomes or stages will dictate both the balance and pacing of your roguelike. A lesson from *Game Design Deep Dive: Platformers* that also fits here is that a good game should go on for as long as the developer can provide new content. Roguelikes are in a special position that having shorter plays is not considered a negative due to the replayability. A necessary element of setting the pace is also determining what the difficulty curve of your roguelike looks like. The game should be getting progressively harder with each new stage, but not so difficult that only a handful of strategies are viable.

When balancing your game along these lines, pay attention to the difficulty increases and whether the design allows players to compensate. A common design trap for pacing is when the jump in terms of enemy difficulty from one area to the next is too high – enemies do 20 points of damage in area 1 to 80 points in area 2. Through playtesting, it is possible to see an average power level that players are going to reach and balance it accordingly. You do not want to balance your game on the notion that the player is going to be overpowered every time, as there is no way of guaranteeing that with content generation.

With *The Binding of Isaac*, the overall difficulty goes up every two stages when the game switches to a new biome. There is a further increase when the player gets to the unlockable harder biomes that remove the treasure room and shop POIs. Until that point, players have the time to hopefully find the items they need to put together a viable strategy for beating the game (Figure 10.4).

The Binding of Isaac also represents another consideration about pacing and balance when it comes to adding in new levels. As mentioned, it has had more endgame content added through its expansions. Normally, roguelikes get additional content in the form of supplemental content discussed in Section 6.4.

The amount of variance with the power level the player could reach in the game meant that there were runs in which nothing in the main game could stop the

Figure 10.4

The Binding of Isaac received length-adding content as well as supplemental, including this hidden final boss fight with delirium.

player, just as there were runs where the player would struggle. Instead of trying to rebalance the game to make it harder for those optimal runs, by adding in the additional content and raising the difficulty in those stages, it provided players with a new challenge to overcome. *Spelunky 2* (released in 2020) has a similar philosophy. After beating the main game, there are additional challenges for expert players to pursue that extend the game's playtime out; including one grandmaster challenge that easily adds several hours to a playthrough.

In effect, it offered players different end points depending on how far they wanted to go. Someone who just barely makes it to the end could stop to get the first ending or push further to get more challenge and a different ending. Due to the progressive nature of roguelike design, it's wise not to make huge waves in terms of adjusting preexisting content balance-wise. Making things too hard will restrict the player's options when some people will not need that difficulty increase. We will be discussing additional difficulty options in Section 10.8 with progressive difficulty.

10.3 Open-World Roguelike Design

Earlier, in Section 6.3, we talked about the three structural formats that roguelikes often make use of: Stage-based, node-based, and open-world. Open-world design is a more advanced – and harder – philosophy when it comes to the roguelike genre.

There are fewer examples of this kind of design, and most of them are roguelite-focused. With this design, the environment is built around multiple biomes with a large focus on POIs. Unlike the other two examples that guide the player, open-world design is more freeform.

The player is free to explore in any direction that suits them to a certain point. Progress is locked either covertly by having stronger enemies as gatekeepers, or overtly by requiring the player to find something or complete a task to move on.

The world design may look more chaotic compared to the other examples, but upon closer inspection it is possible to see the rules of the algorithm at work. Some games will have a fixed size per biome, and then put content in that is spaced out a certain distance (Figure 10.5).

In the game *Sunless Skies* by Failbetter Games (released in 2019), the player explores different areas made up of individual biomes. The biomes are set up so that their general structure is consistent with each play, but their event locations and POIs within them differ. For example, the game will always spawn Biome A west of the starting point, but how far west changes on each playthrough.

One negative of open-world design is that the moment-to-moment gameplay is not as interesting compared to other styles. Due to the size of the game space, players will often spend minutes at a time making the trip from one POI to the next without much happening. The game will place a few enemies or minor events to try and break up the routine, but it does not always work out that way.

The pacing when it comes to actual progress is different here. Other rogue-likes tend to create a structure around a consistent series of events that reward or

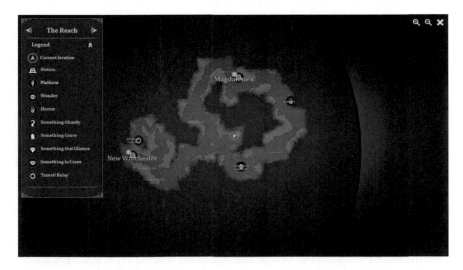

Figure 10.5

In this screenshot from *Sunless Skies*, the world generation of each biome is designed around a general structure, but the actual POIs are shifted with each new playthrough.

challenge the player – finding a treasure room in *Enter the Gungeon* or beating a battle in *Slay the Spire* for instance.

Open-world design is more about peaks and valleys. There will be tasks or the ability to buy and craft new gear that once accomplished will provide the player with a huge boost to their utility. With *Sunless Skies*, the player's first goal is to get enough money so that they can either buy new equipment for their train or buy a new train with greater potential for improvement.

Even though there is no set consistency, having these goals set up and their respective improvements are effective motivators to keep someone playing. Something as simple as increasing general movement speed can be huge in cutting down travel time and can be felt by the player.

Points of interest are also handled differently. Each POI is treated as its own small vignette, and unless they are linked by a story or a previous decision, their functionality and purpose will be entirely self-contained. This could be as simple as finding a food vendor who sells the same items, to a story-driven event of exploring a deserted house.

To win the game, there are two popular options. One: The player must complete specific POIs that either move the story along or unlock the final fight and win. Or two: The player chooses a long-term goal that they must achieve for that play. With *Sunless Skies*, the player sets an ambition at the start of the game, such as earning enough money to retire, that the playthrough will center around. In this respect, open-world design does not have a fixed run length compared to the other examples. Depending on the game, the design may also have some persistent elements that can be carried over. In *Sunless Skies*, players can carry over some resources and unlock new story events on future runs.

Another style of open-world roguelikes is the concept of combining Nintendo's *Legend of Zelda* series (first released in 1986), that is known for the core gameplay loop of exploring the world and growing stronger, with the procedural nature of a roguelike, creating an almost "Zelda-rogue." This kind of design is even more specialized than just making an open-world roguelike. When the world is generated, specific areas will be inaccessible without the right items or upgrades, either hidden throughout the world or in dungeon POIs.

Whatever items are chosen to be included in that run will affect what dungeons and obstacles the game will throw at the player. For example: On one run, the game could generate a bow and arrow that could be used to hit far-away targets and enemies. Potential obstacles could be a locked door with the switch to open it across a gap. A simpler example would be only having a set number of items that could appear, and just shuffling each biome around in terms of where the player can access at the start. Dungeons and POIs can be altered to include specific rooms/obstacles that take advantage of the specific items that were chosen for the run (Figure 10.6).

There are only a handful of titles that have gone this route, and the one that took this concept the furthest in my opinion was *The Swords of Ditto* by One Bit Beyond in 2018. Each run generated different items, dungeons, and changed

Figure 10.6

In every run of the *Swords of Ditto*, there will always be two dungeons, each containing an item that the rest of the traps and obstacles will be balanced around.

the overworld. While the game did have persistence (that also factored into the story), each run was a self-contained adventure with a different pool of quest-required items to find and use.

The common issue that plagues most open-world roguelikes comes down to their moment-to-moment gameplay. Too much of the game space is just fluff, and the player's attention is once again on the POIs. No matter how the world is generated, progress is still only defined by a handful of fixed elements. As discussed in Section 6.1, shuffling elements around in a procedurally generated space does not create variance between runs. If the major goals remain fixed, the player will just repeat the same steps for each run.

When a game has too much of a focus on fixed content, it tends to hurt the game's ability to create variance, and we will be discussing this further in Section 10.5.

10.4 The Focal Points of Replayability

We have discussed at length in this book about replayability and variance, and for the next three sections, I want to summarize what aspects affect, and can limit, the replayability of a game. The reason why this is important is that roguelikes live or die based on how replayable they are.

The replay value of a roguelike comes down to three distinct areas that the content generation should impact:

1. What is the goal?
2. What are the player's tools?
3. What is standing in the player's way?

The goal means different things depending on the design of the roguelike. In *Spelunky*, "the goal" is making it to the exit door in each stage, while in *FTL*, the player must cross a map to enter the next sector.

Goals in roguelikes are often fixed events, as the structure of the game is built from them. There are ways to affect the goal without altering its purpose. In *Slay the Spire*, there is always a boss fight at the top of each level, but the game randomly chooses from a pool of possible fights on each playthrough. *The Binding of Isaac* with its expansions also added in more bosses to the pool that could show up on any floor outside of the floors where there were set fights.

An easier to design option is to simply change the position of the goal or exit when generating an area (such as in traditional roguelikes). While this does help, it does not affect what the player is going to be doing to get to it. Speaking of what the player is doing, the tools are the items, new abilities, equipment, etc., that can show up during a run to aid them.

For this category, we are ignoring the basic moveset and options the player has access to because they are foundational for every run. Depending on the design, it is possible to create items that have major impacts on playing. Once again, the variety of items in *The Binding of Isaac* is the best example (Figure 10.7).

If there is not enough item variety, then the game will become repetitive. In *Spelunky*, most runs will end with the same set of items each time, as the item pool is on the smaller side. A far worse problem is if there are too many items, but only a select few that aid the player.

Figure 10.7

The variety of the player's tools, and their interactions between one another, are a major source of variance and depth to a game's design.

For tools to have an impact on variance, they cannot provide the same benefit or utility as a preexisting tool. Going back to our list of categories of content in Section 6.2, if the game already has a category of one-handed weapons that behave the same way, adding in 50 more with an expansion will not change the experience. POIs can count in this category if they provide a new benefit for the player. Some action roguelikes and roguelites have added in new events with updates designed to aid the player.

Deck-building roguelikes have an advantage when it comes to their cards. The impact and utility of a new card in a game like *Monster Train* or *Slay the Spire* can radically change the player's strategy, and how cards can interact with one another. You do not need anywhere near the same number of items in a deck builder compared to action roguelikes if each card is unique in terms of utility. In any roguelike, it should not be possible to collect every item in the game, and this is especially true of deck builders that are often designed around a fixed number of battles.

As a design point, it is important to decide early on how the various tools interact with one another. Some games, like *The Binding of Isaac*, allow item effects to stack, which can lead to overpowered options. Other games will say that the strongest effect the player has will be the active one and will override the weaker options. From the player's perspective, it is more interesting to be able to combine options and find those overpowered combinations.

The final category, what is standing in the player's way, is one that is either quite easy, or awfully hard, to do given the design of the title. This category includes enemies obviously, but it also includes environmental obstacles: Pits, spikes, lava, rotating blades, and anything else that the player will have to actively avoid during play.

The reason why this can be difficult to do properly is that obstacle difficulty is connected to the player's ability. In *Spelunky*, each biome only has a small number of obstacles that can show up. Regardless of the hazard, the player will often have a few ways to get around it. Once the player knows how to get around it, that solution will work every time and in every run.

What happens then is that the obstacles in the game simply become window dressing in the level. Expert play in *Dead Cells* works the same way: No matter how the levels are generated and where enemies and hazards are placed, the player is going to move through them the same way every time.

For traditional roguelikes, a popular obstacle to use is a trap. A trap is an invisible object that the player will only detect if their character has the right attributes, or they set it off. Once triggered, the trap will perform an effect: Explode, weaken the player, drop them down a floor, etc.

One way of keeping things interesting is to introduce the idea of "elite" variations of enemies. These versions will look different, usually just a color palette change, and have an added property to fighting them: Increased damage, moving faster, generating minions, etc. Killing them can often yield higher rewards compared to the normal versions, and the game can be set to generate them at random intervals (Figure 10.8).

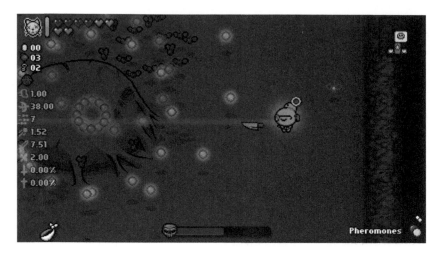

Figure 10.8

The Binding of Isaac introduced new enemy types, new bosses, and new elite variations, through its expansions to add more diverse challenges alongside new items and events.

Another option has to do with changing the player's tools on each run which affects how they must deal with the obstacles. This has been one of the major advantages of deck-builder roguelikes when it comes to variance. The encounters in games like *Monster Train* or *Slay the Spire* are handmade, but the player does not know which exact ones they are getting in a play (or when they will show up in a run). When this is combined with the dynamic that the player's deck (or their options) in each run will be different, it means there is no way to create a set strategy that works every time.

Within these three categories, developers have a lot of space to play around with ways of creating variance. There must always be enough content created that the game can keep making new runs to challenge the player. I have personally played several roguelikes that were released without enough content and was getting repeats of floor layouts and equipment within the first couple of runs.

If your goal is to create a roguelite and you are not focused as much on long-term replayability, then this is not the worst problem in the world, but do not expect people to be playing your game for dozens of runs.

10.5 The Dangers of Fixed Content

Videogames regardless of their genre are designed around "anchor points" that give them structure – having a boss at the end of a stage, finding upgrades, and many more examples.

These anchors become fixed events within the game that a player can always rely on occurring during play. For roguelikes or any game with replayability, fixed content is the complete anthesis of variance.

There are two aspects of fixed content we need to discuss, and we will start with events themselves. In the last section we went over the areas that impact replayability. If a roguelike is structured so rigidly that the player knows what will happen each time, that will ruin any chance at creating variance.

When games have fixed elements, a **meta** is formed. Metas are popular strategies that are at the time of their creation the best ways of playing a game. Gamers and developers often talk about them in multiplayer titles when a certain strategy or item becomes the best option. For the roguelike genre, the more predictable a game becomes can impact the difficulty. If the player knows that X will always happen, they can prepare for that event and mitigate its impact.

What is worse is when fixed elements create difficulty. Games that allow the player to customize how they play are set up to introduce "builds," which is a way of describing a set of abilities or options that work well together, for example, having a bonus to bleed damage and then finding weapons and spells that can cause it (Figure 10.9).

One of the best parts of RPGs can be the **customization** system that allows the player to fully create a character, or characters, to play the game with. Customization, along with **personalization** (changing the look of a character), allows players to feel more connected to the character and world. The use of customization also creates greater depth for players who challenge themselves with finding the best ways of playing.

However, the more options available to the player means there must be ways for those options to work. If the player creates a fire build (or finds nothing but

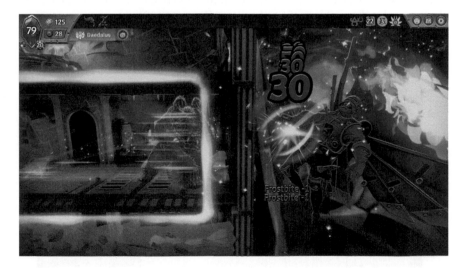

Figure 10.9

Builds are strategies that are created based on the options the player has access to and their overall effectiveness. Here, my strategy was to boost my monster to hit harder, strike first, and punch multiple times per round, to overpower the enemies.

fire weapons) and one section of the game is nothing but fire-immune enemies, then that build, and the respective parts of it, are worthless. A common trope of many early RPGs was giving the player a variety of status-effecting spells but finding out that bosses are completely immune to them, making them worthless for those encounters. When a meta becomes established in any game, it reduces all choice down to the best options in the game, everything else being second.

We can also see metas if a game has pacing issues discussed in Section 10.2. A run could be over before it even started if the player knows that a fixed event is coming up that requires a certain item or a power level to be reached. As mentioned, this is why you need to figure out a baseline of how strong the player should grow over the course of the run and try to avoid any sharp increases of difficulty.

Monster Train is a good example of playing around with variance within a fixed structure of events. At the start of a run, the player chooses two factions that determine what cards and items will show up. They are then told what variation of the final boss they will fight. Each version was designed to counter specific strategies. From there, the player must figure out a solution given their factions and what cards and events will show up. Good balance dictates that everything should be good in a specific situation, with nothing being the best at any time, and we will talk more about this concept in Section 10.7.

From the designer's point of view, the goal is to create an experience that is fixed enough that the game knows what to build, while still leaving things open-ended enough to accommodate different strategies and create variance. With that said, even if a game starts with hundreds of items, POIs, and obstacles, that does not solve the problem of fixed content (Figure 10.10).

Figure 10.10

Gwent went through multiple redesigns of its gameplay, balancing existing cards, and adding in new ones, to reach the state that it is in now.

The second element of fixed content has to do with the content itself. While roguelikes can be designed to produce an infinite number of game spaces, they are still using a handmade pool created by the developer, meaning that eventually players will see everything the game has to offer from a variance point of view. The only solutions are to either constantly change existing content or add new content.

Returning to Section 6.1 and variance, simply filling the environment with content is not enough to create variance. Once again, the goal is to provide the player with unique and different experiences for each run generated. Eventually astute players will know all the major events and situations that will appear in a game. This is a consistent problem for multiplayer designers when it comes to competitive titles – no matter how many fighters there are in a game, cards or deck strategies, or weapons to choose from, a fixed number of options will always lead to the generation of a meta.

A solidified meta is the nightmare scenario for competitive titles, and why the work is never finished for these games. Multiplayer designers must rebalance their games and add in content on a regular basis to maintain their games. Fortunately for roguelike developers the stakes are not as high. The phenomenon we described can take dozens, or even hundreds, of hours of play depending on the scope of the game.

With all that said, it is time to bust a certain myth around replayability.

10.6 Debunking "Infinite Replayability"

The last decade once again saw the rise of roguelike games and the philosophy of live-service games in the mainstream market. A term that has been thrown around by people is this idea of "infinite replayability" – that a game, given enough content and updates, can be played forever.

As someone who covers videogames for a living, I have lost count of the number of games marketed to have infinite replayability, to find that the actual game is anything but. While replayability is important for any roguelike, it is not the only reason to play them. Procgen will not fix poor controls or imbalanced gameplay. That reason is why amazing roguelikes are hard to do right – as the game design must be great to then be broken down and remade using the content generation.

There are certainly games out there that have maintained fans and have been kept alive for years. We already spoke about roguelikes like *Nethack*, but there are live-service games that are still going. For MMOs, there is *World of Warcraft* by Blizzard Studios, which was originally released in 2004. The game that took off and became a major spark for live-service design would be *League of Legends* by Riot Games in 2009.

Long-lasting is not the same as infinite, and as a designer, it is important to understand that there are two inherent limits in any game. The first is the very fact that a videogame is built on handmade assets. As we have discussed, procgen – no matter how complex and powerful it may be – does not create original work

Figure 10.11

Live service games that succeed in the market tend to have amazing replay value. This is due to the continued support and additional content added for years to come.

(Figure 10.11). Regardless of how much content is created for the game to use, there is always a limit on the amount of variance any game can have. This is a similar phenomenon to meta builds in games. Once the player has seen all the major aspects of a game, they can then start to figure out the best strategies based on the pool of possibilities.

An important point to reiterate for the games mentioned above is that each one has been receiving updates with new content added. For *World of Warcraft* and *League of Legends,* they would not still be played to this day without their live-service approach. For roguelikes, without having new content that the game can use for its generation, the player will reach a point when they have seen all the major events the game has to offer.

You may be thinking, "why don't I just add more to my game?" Unfortunately, that takes us to the other point: Eventually any designer will run out of ideas for new content. That is not meant to insult game developers; it is just the nature of building a game.

Therefore, many roguelikes feature **modding** support: Allowing fans to create new content and rules for other players to download. While it may not approach infinity, this is the next best thing to it. In some cases, mods can become so popular that the developer may decide to integrate content or features into the base game, as with the case of several *Binding of Isaac* mods.

I know this point has been hammered in, but we need to say it one last time: Procgen does not fix the bad design. Even if you do become the exception and create a roguelike with infinite replayability, if it is built off a poorly designed game, then no one will care about all that infinity.

10.7 Balancing the Unpredictable

In Section 6.5, we discussed the topic of balancing a game around random and procedural content, but there is more to this point when it comes to roguelikes. A common design problem seen in roguelikes is about balancing the fixed nature of events (from Section 10.5) with the unpredictable nature of content generation.

Games that are built on RPG-based systems of progression will often challenge the player to find the best upgrades or gear during the playthrough. The problem occurs if the requirements for success are too narrow and the player is doomed before they even start playing.

In *FTL*, the final challenge is a three-stage fight with the rebel flagship. This is a fixed event with the ship changing its tactics and options at each stage. To win, the player must find over the length of the playthrough the right upgrades and weapons that can successfully counter the ship at each stage. If the player fails to find an answer for all three, then the run will end with a loss and is an example of fixed content that we discussed two sections ago.

This issue can often be compounded when games add in more supplemental content in the form of new equipment. From Section 6.2, adding more options to your categories gives the game more choices when it comes to deciding what to generate, but it also decreases the player's chance of getting what they need (Figure 10.12).

For example, let us say that there is a roguelike that has 30 different items that could appear during a play. Of those 30, 5 items provide the player with the only way to heal easily, which due to the design is an important part of beating the game. Doing some quick math, that comes out to a 16.7% chance that the player

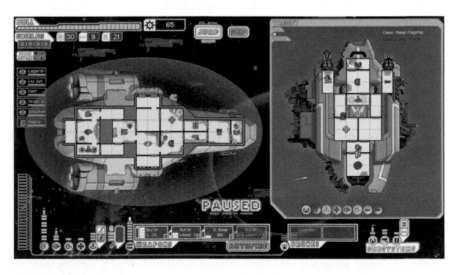

Figure 10.12

The rebel flagship of FTL is an example of a fixed fight with only a handful of viable solutions for each of its phases.

will get one of those items in a single run. If the developer releases an update that adds in 30 more items – none of them providing the player with the ability to heal – the chance that the player is going to get what they need drops to 8.3%.

Trying to calculate the success rate of a run gets even harder when we factor in player skill. In the previous example, we are assuming that the player is going to take damage and will require some form of healing. There is the possibility that there will be players who are so good at the game that they will not need healing, and not require those items to win. As the developer, you need to decide on the level of skill required to be able to win, and that is where the **skill ceiling** comes in.

Roguelikes of all shapes and forms must walk a careful line in terms of how to win. The game should not be so easy that someone can fumble through and win, nor should it be so difficult that only the top 5% of the player base can finish it. The more demanding a game is in terms of player skill will limit the fanbase. However, there are fans of games who only play difficult titles.

The problem is that it is impossible as the designer to know exactly what the player is going to get in any given run and balance the difficulty accordingly. Therefore, you need to pay special attention to items or options that have specialized roles. Going back to the healing example, let us say that now there are 2 items out of 30 that the final boss is weak against, turning a difficult final fight into a cakewalk. Doing the math, that comes out to a 0.67 chance of getting those items. For lesser skilled players who do not have the skills otherwise to win, they are going to lose 99.33% of the time. For the expert players, they may not see any problem with having such a low chance, because they are already good enough at the game to not require those items.

The solution that we have seen from roguelike designers is to focus on creating specific builds or strategies that can be powered up to give the player a win. In *Monster Train*, within the two factions that the player chooses at the start there are multiple build combinations. No matter the strategy the player picks, every build has one goal: Do enough damage to beat the final boss before it beats them.

When you are examining the balance of your game, look at the actual viable ways to win, and see how many items, builds, or POIs can facilitate a win state. With the *Monster Train* example, one faction has the special ability to put spikes on their characters that cause damage whenever that character is struck. In this regard, the player is still on the hunt for "damage," but a different kind of damage compared to other builds. The spike build can be supplemented with specific artifacts or by upgrading the cards to make them better, and the same goes for every other build in the game.

I personally like describing balance in randomized or procedurally generated titles as that there should not be a choice that is the best all the time, but every choice should have its moment in the sun. It is always better from the user's point of view to boost lesser options than weaken an already viable option. Nobody likes to see a strategy or style of play they like become less effective (Figure 10.13).

With that said, if something is so good that it becomes the best choice in every situation, that might be a case to reduce its effectiveness. Conversely, if

Figure 10.13

In this scene from *Slay the Spire*, I am committed to a discard-based build due to the cards that showed up, and I am trying to find more cards that synergize with it.

something is so bad that no one wants to take it in any situation, that could mean buffing that option.

Games that procedurally generate items or gear, such as action roguelikes and ARPGs, become a little harder to balance. Essentially, every item in the game is made up of two parts: The base properties that define the item, and what modifiers could show up on it. As the designer, you should look at both parts separately when it comes to balancing the game.

In *Dead Cells*' case, the developers went over their items to see if there were specific ones that people didn't like to use for whatever reason, and looked at the modifiers to see if they were providing a good enough benefit to aid the player. One example was changing certain passive abilities in terms of their use of fixed numbers vs. percentages.

A major aspect of balancing options is the difference between fixed numbers and percentages. If a weapon or player skill provides the player with a fixed damage rating – the attack does 37 points of damage for instance – that ability will lose its utility the longer the game goes on due to the increased scaling of enemy stats. A better option is to balance options based on a percentage of the character's overall stats – the attack will do 56% of the character's attack stat. The difference is that the latter will improve naturally as the character becomes more powerful. While percentage-base works for games with procedural content, for games built on fixed content and options (like deck builders), fixed-number design is the preferred way to balance.

You are never going to achieve perfect balance in any game with procedurally generated situations, but that is also the charm of these games. The goal is to provide an experience so that the player can understand the overall goal but to keep them on their toes with what happens. Someone should never be able to tell how a run is going to play out. There can be runs that are doomed from the start, runs that begin and end as a cakewalk, and every variation in-between.

While mastery and skill at the game can mitigate the randomness to some extent, there will always come a time when the player is going to lose, and there was nothing they could do to stop it. When that happens, your first thought may be: "is my game broken, do I need to fix this?" It is important to take a step back and see how often this is occurring. There is a huge difference between someone losing because of a player mistake, and someone losing before they even started playing.

Playtesting can help to see if there are any choices that are not balanced, and developers can make use of public or private testers.

10.8 Progressive Difficulty

Difficulty has been one of the cornerstones of roguelike design since its inception, for better and worse. The genre has always been challenging to get into for non-fans, let alone how easy it is to lose due to bad luck. A relatively new system that we have seen is the idea of progressive difficulty. Instead of using persistent elements as a form of content and growth, progressive difficulty applies that philosophy to the difficulty of the game itself (Figure 10.14).

Due to the run-by-run focus of traditional roguelikes, it would be a harder fit for them to include progressive difficulty, but they do have some options. Some

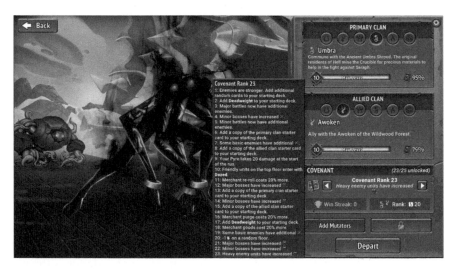

Figure 10.14

Progressive difficulty requires balance at all levels, and that must be weighed against the options the player has, as they will not be changing.

roguelikes have featured a "challenge mode" that expert players can turn on that increases the difficulty in some way. This can be tied to a leaderboard or ranking system to see who is the best under that specific modifier.

The first major example of progressive difficulty would be *Slay the Spire* and its "ascension mode." When someone starts playing the game for the first time, the difficulty is set at level 0 – essentially the game at its easiest and balanced state. Playing the game like this, level 0 would provide challenge and test players as they learn how to play. Someone could mess up and still have a good chance at winning.

After getting a win, the game begins to unlock its ascension and allow the player to replay a run at difficulty level 1. Unlike traditional difficulty settings that provide blanket changes to a game on each level, each individual level of progressive difficulty changes the game in one way. This could be increasing the price of buying items at a shop, introducing unhelpful cards that the player starts with, and of course: Raising the attributes of enemies.

Each level essentially "layers" the difficulty on top of itself and challenges the player to adapt. Not every change directly increases the difficulty. Raising shop prices does not change the function or options there, but it is a way of forcing the player to change their strategy going forward. The only way to unlock the next level up is to have a successful run at the current maxed level reached. Playing *Slay the Spire*, or any game with progressive difficulty at the highest level, should be the absolute hardest, *but still winnable*, version of the game. Progressive difficulty is like the concept of a new game plus mode: When the player can replay the game with everything harder. The difference is that progressive difficulty is suited for the focus on runs of a roguelike.

What makes progressive difficulty work so well for roguelike games is that it integrates the difficulty of the game into the progression and learning curve. In effect, it allows developers to have their cake and eat it too, in a sense. The game can start off on the easier side to allow new players a chance to get accustomed to it, while still providing expert players with increased challenges and goals to achieve.

Progressive difficulty can be related to weightlifting and continuing to add weights until someone reaches their limit. Not everyone is going to want to play a game at the highest difficulty level, just as there are going to be people who will get to the top and stay there. The beauty of progressive difficulty is that the game accommodates all player styles and assures that fans will be able to get something out of the game no matter what level they stop playing.

The player is the one who is deciding how far they want to be challenged and can play the game at their own pace. Allowing someone to control the difficulty of the game makes it more approachable and is better than just having blanket difficulty settings. The problem with traditional difficulty is that raising or lowering it may not impact the part of the game the player wants to change (Figure 10.15).

An advanced version of progressive difficulty can be seen in the game *Hades* by Supergiant Games, released in 2020. To unlock additional rewards, the player must turn on different modifiers to the difficulty and gameplay. Each modifier changes

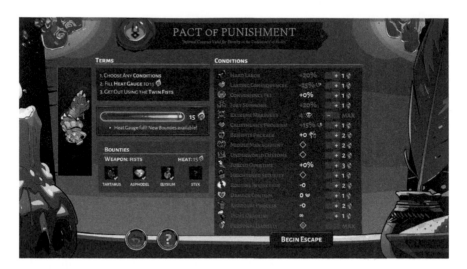

Figure 10.15

Hade's "Pact of Punishment" progressive difficulty system is the current most advanced version of the design. As the player is the one who decides how high they want to go for rewards, and what modifiers to turn on.

some aspect of the game – increasing trap damage, adding a time limit to playing, reducing healing, and so on. The modifiers have a different point value associated with them in terms of their impact on the game. Provided the player hits the difficulty threshold for the next set of rewards, they are free to mix and match however they see fit. Player-controlled difficulty is a philosophy and system that is gaining traction in terms of UX design and not just in roguelikes.

With everything said however, progressive difficulty does present its own challenges when it comes to game balance. Due to the modifiers being added on top of each other, this means a game must be balanced and designed for every level or modifier choice. In effect, a game like *Slay the Spire* is really 20 differently balanced games in one package.

The higher someone raises the progressive difficulty, the less of a safety net they have available. Builds or strategies that are not considered top tier lose viability or become outright useless at the higher levels. The margin of error, or being able to mitigate bad luck, shrinks considerably, and only the best strategies will have a chance. From a design standpoint, progressive difficulty requires a careful eye on the options and tactics that the player can use. What the player has access to will not change regardless of the level of difficulty, but their impact and viability will. Therefore, changing the attributes of enemies as the difficulty increases needs to be handed carefully to keep in step with the player (Figure 10.16).

For example, let us say the player's basic attack does 5 points of damage and enemies at progressive difficulty 0 have 10 points of health, meaning it takes 2 attacks to defeat an enemy and limit the damage they do to the player. Now, let us

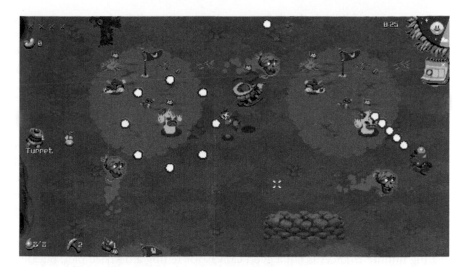

Figure 10.16

Progressive difficulty has the effect of tightening up the ways to win, and sometimes a perfect run may be required at the highest settings.

raise the difficulty level up to 5 and enemies now start with 25 points of health, requiring 5 hits from the player to perform the same task and they will take damage fighting them.

You would assume that to fix balance issues, buffing the player would work, but it is not that simple. Remember, balance with progressive difficulty must consider every level of it, including the starting one. If something is top tier at level 0, buffing it further to compensate for higher levels will just make it imbalanced. Going back to the previous section, every choice should be viable, given the right circumstance.

The RNG of games with progressive difficulty becomes a larger factor as the player's winning options shrink. In both *Monster Train* and *Slay the Spire*, the player must have a solid deck and strategy early in a run to start building toward, or they will not be able to keep up with the increasingly dangerous enemies.

Roguelikes are often built on the core gameplay loop that the player's character is always getting stronger, and early advantages can often lead to wins. Conversely, not starting off with a good strategy or lucky items makes it harder to win and often leads to a downward spiral of losing. In the game *Atomicrops* by Bird Bath Games, released in 2020, there are ten levels of progressive difficulty. At the highest level, enemies are several times faster, take more damage, and the screen is full of projectiles the player must always dodge. If the player is not able to get powerful items and resources from the very beginning, everything progress-related slows down, making it less likely they will be able to win due to the length of a run. This issue is magnified when it comes to the stricter win conditions present at higher persistent levels.

The number of difficulty levels for a game's progressive difficulty system depends on how many modifiers can be added without making the game unplayable. As mentioned, even at the highest difficulty level designed, the game should still be winnable. Finally, when it comes to adjusting different levels, try to work your way from low to high, as every level affects the balance of the subsequent levels.

10.9 Narrative Roguelikes

For our final section, I want to turn to a topic that is not normally associated with roguelikes: The story. There is a larger discussion around the often-polarized forces of story and game design, and the concept of **ludonarrative dissonance** that is too big to get into here and often causes groaning among developers. The short version is that game mechanics often conflict with the storytelling and plot of a title and can lead to this dissonance when it comes to combining them.

For roguelikes, a game that is meant to be replayed endlessly with the player having infinite chances is not a good canvas for telling a detailed plot, but that does not make it impossible. There have been games with roguelike elements that lean into the design when crafting their narrative and setting (Figure 10.17).

An easy example would be *Rogue Legacy* that frames death and rebirth as simply moving to the next generation of heroes to tackle the game's dungeon. The cycle of living and dying was embraced fully in both *Demon's* and *Dark Souls*. In *Demon's Souls*, the player character is killed and turned into a spirit from the outset: Allowing them to die and come back as often as they want. *Dark Souls'* plot is more involved and has to do with the world going through a cycle of death

Figure 10.17

It is rare to see a roguelike that not only refers to its roguelike nature, but integrates that directly into the storytelling.

and rebirth, and the player's character is an undead being cursed to keep coming back until they can move the cycle forward.

It is not often to see a game reference the player's actual or narrative-breaking immortality, and *Hades* is an exception. The player controls the son of Hades, who is a demigod and immortal trying to escape from Hades. Every other main character in the game is immortal, and they frequently reference previous encounters and the fact that the main character continues to try and break out.

For traditional roguelikes, the most common example is that with each game the player is creating a new hero to take on the game's quest and dying simply means that character has failed and someone else must take their place.

Even though the story is not often the part that developers focus on, being able to combine the narrative and gameplay leads to stronger titles and helps consumers connect more to the experience. For the designers reading this, do not be afraid to explore this space. Another avenue is to focus on world building and creating a compelling setting. In *Monster Train*, every card, enemy, and artifact has lore associated with it – fleshing out the world beyond just the gameplay.

Failbetter Games are known for their storytelling and lore and tend to create POIs in their games with unique short stories. This modular approach allows them to update their games with additional storytelling and events that are supplemental to the gameplay.

Combining storytelling and roguelike gameplay has been one area where the newer action roguelikes and roguelites have been doing more compared to traditional examples. And as more developers continue to adopt and explore roguelike elements, I am sure this trend will continue.

Conclusion

It has been fascinating to see the growth of roguelikes and all its subcategories over the last decade. Of all the game genres, the variety (and arguments) of its design stand out. Traditional roguelikes are being developed more around approachability and elevating their design even further. And newer developers are experimenting with the design and taking it to places no one thought the genre could go.

Even at its basic elements, roguelike design is like a spice that can be implemented into other genres – either elevating them when done right or hurting the experience if done wrong. The best part? As we have seen with examples like *Prey Mooncrash* and *Bloodborne* implementing roguelike elements, even AAA games can explore roguelike design to some capacity. Many of the modern roguelikes mentioned in this book were created by taking an aspect of roguelike design and doing something else with it beyond the original conventions set. Do not be afraid to experiment and remember: There's no shame in having your game be called a roguelite.

Procedural generation, when done right, has a lot of potential for games not just in the roguelike genre. Again, if you are interested more in content generation, be sure to read *Procedural Generation in Game Design*. There is still plenty of untapped possibilities for the use of procedural generation, but it must be handled properly.

I hope that this book has helped you in terms of understanding the complexities that go with the genre, as so much of what makes it work lies under the surface. I cannot wait to see what new takes on roguelike, roguelite, or any other "likes" developers come up with over the next decade.

Glossary

AAA: In the game industry it is used to describe major studios such as Nintendo and Electronic Arts who put out the biggest and most expensive games each year.

Abstraction: How videogames will represent events and actions in a game separate from real-life analogs.

Action roguelike: A variation of the roguelike genre that features procedural generation and a run-by-run focus but is not designed around turn-based gameplay.

Aesthetics: The emotion or style that the game's art and sound try to convey.

AI: Short for "artificial intelligence" and represents the game-controlling or game-directing obstacles or non-playable characters.

Algorithm: A sequence of instructions for a computer to use. For roguelikes, it represents the rules and procedure the game will use when procedurally generating content.

Approachability: How easy a game makes it for new players to get in and start enjoying playing it; often discussed with onboarding.

ARPG: Short for "action role-playing game" and is a genre where players control their characters directly, but still has a heavy influence of RPG design and character building.

ASCII: Short for "American Standard Code for Information Interchange." Built as a way of representing the alphabet as numbers for computers to understand. Used by roguelike developers as a way of creating the game space without needing to create art assets.

Assets: The elements made by the designer or team that the game is built from.

Biome: For videogames, a grouping of all content (enemies, POIs, etc.) that can appear in a specific environment.

Buff: Used to describe making something in a game stronger or better.

CCG: Short for "collectible card game," a type of game played with cards either on a real or digital board.

Character: Whoever the player is controlling directly in a game; can also be referred to as an in-game avatar.

Core gameplay loop: The main system or interaction that the player will spend most of their time doing.

Customization: Refers to any aspects of their character(s) that the player can change that will impact how the game is played with them.

DLC: Short for "downloadable content" and represents additional content the player can buy and get access to after a game's release.

Dynamic: Used to describe the interactions between mechanics of the same, or different, systems of a game.

Emergent gameplay: A form of gameplay that allows the player to create their own solutions and methods of play beyond the original function of the mechanics.

Free to play: Games that have no upfront cost to play but earn their money through in-game transactions.

Gameplay: Used to describe what the player is doing when playing a game.

Game space: The environment or world that the game takes place in.

GUI: Short for "graphical user interface" and represents all the onscreen elements that provide the player with information about what is happening in the game.

Hardcore: A way of playing games where the player's character is erased if they die during play; also referred to as permadeath.

JRPG: Short for "Japanese role-playing game" and is a part of the RPG genre. Used to describe RPGs where the player uses predefined characters with their own story as opposed to making their own.

Kaizo: A Japanese term loosely meaning reorganize, has become the way of describing brutally difficult platformers where there is only one exact way of winning.

Live service: A model of releasing and marketing a game with continued support and development after release to keep people invested and spending money on new content.

Loot table: An algorithm specifically for defining how the game will procedurally generate equipment that the player can find; often used in ARPGs and RPGs.

Ludonarrative dissonance: A term to describe the disconnect between the storytelling and gameplay of a videogame.

Mechanic: A way of describing the actions, or verbs, that someone will do while playing a game.

Meta: Whatever is the most popular/powerful option currently in a game and is often talked about in multiplayer-based games.

Metroidvania: A 2D subgenre where the abilities and options of controlling a character grow and change over the playthrough.

Modding/mods: Modifiers for games that are often created by fans that can be shared either through the game itself, or from third-party sites. Modding is the act of creating mods.

Onboarding: For videogames, it is the process in which a game will teach someone how to play it.

Open world: A type of game that is not structured around beating levels but completing objectives in an open space.

PBEM: Short for "play by email" and is a way of having multiple people play a game without direct interaction at the same time.

Permadeath: A way of describing a game where the player's character is permanently deleted when they are killed in-game.

Persistence: Elements or systems that carry over between the runs of a roguelike to provide long-term or permanent changes to how the game is played.

Personalization: Refers to any aspects that the player can change about their character(s) in terms of how they look, without affecting the gameplay.

Player: The person playing the videogame.

Points of interest: Self-contained events set up in videogames with a specific purpose or function to help or hinder the player.

Procedural generation: Also known as procgen, a form of content generation where the game will build something new out of preexisting assets.

Progression curve: How either the player themselves or their character makes progress in the game.

Progressive difficulty: A difficulty system that adds new modifiers or conditions each time the player wins to make the game more challenging for expert players.

Random number generator: Also known as RNG, a form of content generation where the game will decide the result of an event from a fixed pool of possible outcomes.

Real-time: A way of referring to games where everything is happening at the same time and is often used to describe the differences between strategy games.

Replayability: Used to describe if a game has enough content or reason to be replayed after finishing it.

Roguelike: A game genre that is made up of multiple subgenres. The standard version focuses on turn-based combat with a focus on procedural generation and permadeath with each run being a clean slate.

Roguelite: A variation of roguelike design that keeps the procedural generation and restarting on failure, but is focused on long-term play and carryover between runs.

RPG: Short for "role-playing game," a genre that focuses on character building and in-game attributes as opposed to player reflexes with many different takes and subgenres.

Skill ceiling: The highest amount of skill required by the player to beat the game.

Soulslike/souls-like: A description of games that base their design elements and gameplay on the hit *Dark Souls* series by From Software.

Spawn: A term used to describe when the game places or creates something in the world.

System: A way of categorizing and grouping similar mechanics together, such as a jumping or fighting system.

Subgenre: A subcategory of a game genre with unique differences or qualifiers that separate it from other examples in the genre.

Supplemental content: A form of content added to a game that increases the variance and replayability without impacting the average length of a play.

Turn-based: A form of gameplay where the game is played out in the form of turns as opposed to everything happening in real time.

UI: Short for "user interface" and encompassing everything that has to do with how someone interacts with a game.

UX: Short for "user experience" and describes how someone feels when playing a videogame.

Variance: A way of describing what actual mechanics or systems in a game will make it replayable.

Index

Storytelling, 43, 61, 94, 95
Subset Games, 50
Sunless Skies (2019), 77, 78
Supergiant Games, 91
Super Mario 64 (1996), 59, 69
Supplemental content, 37–39, 75, 87
The Surge series (2017), 61
The Swords of Ditto (2018), 78

Tabletop-based games, 20
Tharsis (2016), 22
Toejam and Earl (1991), 13–14
Toy, Michael, 4
Turn-based design, 7–8, 14, 46, 55–56, 64
Turn-based system, 5

UI, *see* User interface
"Ultra Nightmare," 11
Umoira, see Moira (1983)

User experience (UX) design, 56, 68, 72, 73, 92
User interface (UI), 23, 24, 68, 72, 73
UX, *see* User experience design

Variance, 32, 34, 35, 40, 46–48, 51, 56, 61, 62, 64, 67, 74–75, 79, 81, 82, 84

Weapons, 33, 60
"We-Go" system, 7, 8, 48
Whalen, Peter, 52
Wichman, Glenn, 4
Wizards of the Coast, 52
World of Warcraft (2004), 85, 86

XCOM 2 (2012), 22, 38
XCOM franchise (1994), 7–8, 22

Yu, Derek, 46